Teen-agers and Sex

INQUIRY INTO CRUCIAL AMERICAN PROBLEMS

Series Editor · JACK R. FRAENKEL

Teen-agers and Sex:

Revolution or Reaction?

JACK L. NELSON

Professor of Education (Social Sciences)
Rutgers University

PRENTICE-HALL, INC. ENGLEWOOD CLIFFS, N.J.

Titles in this series:

CRIME AND CRIMINALS: What Should We Do About Them?
Jack R. Fraenkel

PREJUDICE AND DISCRIMINATION: Can We Eliminate Them?
Fred R. Holmes

THE DRUG SCENE: Help or Hang-up?
Walter L. Way

POVERTY IN AN AFFLUENT SOCIETY: Personal Problem or National Disgrace?
David A. Durfee

COUNTRY, CONSCIENCE, AND CONSCRIPTION: Can They Be Reconciled?
Leo A. Bressler and Marion A. Bressler

VOICES OF DISSENT: Positive Good or Disruptive Evil?
Frank Kane

CITIES IN CRISIS: Decay or Renewal?
Rudie W. Tretten

TEEN-AGERS AND SEX: Revolution or Reaction?
Jack L. Nelson

PROPAGANDA, POLLS, AND PUBLIC OPINION: Are the People Manipulated?
Malcolm G. Mitchell

ALIENATION: Individual or Social Problem?
Ronald V. Urick

EDUCATION AND OPPORTUNITY: For What and For Whom?
Gordon M. Seely

FOREIGN POLICY: Intervention, Involvement, or Isolation?
Alvin Wolf

Printed in the United States of America

ISBN 0-13-902288-0 paper
ISBN 0-13-902304-6 cloth

1 2 3 4 5 6 7 8 9 10

Prentice-Hall International, Inc., *London*
Prentice-Hall of Australia, Pty. Ltd., *Sydney*
Prentice-Hall of Canada, Ltd., *Toronto*
Prentice-Hall of India Private Ltd., *New Delhi*
Prentice-Hall of Japan, Inc., *Tokyo*

PREFACE

The series *INQUIRY INTO CRUCIAL AMERICAN PROBLEMS* focuses upon a number of important contemporary social and political issues. Each book presents an in-depth study of a particular problem, selected because of its pressing intrusion into the minds and consciences of most Americans today. A major concern has been the desire to make the materials relevant to students. Every title in the series, therefore, has been selected because, in one way or another, it suggests a problem of concern to students today.

A number of divergent viewpoints, from a wide variety of different *kinds* of sources, encourage discussion and reflection and illustrate that the same problem may be viewed from many different vantage points. Of concern throughout is a desire to help students realize that honest men may legitimately differ in their views.

After a short chapter introducing the questions with which the book will deal, Chapter 2 presents a brief historical and contemporary background so that students will have more than just a superficial understanding of the problem under study. In the readings that follow, a conscientious effort has been made to avoid endorsing any one viewpoint as the "right" viewpoint, or to evaluate the arguments of particular individuals. No conclusions are drawn. Instead, a number of questions for discussion and reflection are posed at the end of each reading so that students can come to their own conclusions.

Great care has been taken to insure that the readings included in each book are just that—readable! We have searched particularly for articles that are of high interest, yet from which differing viewpoints may be legitimately inferred. Whenever possible, dialogues involving or descriptions showing actual people responding and reacting to problematic situations are presented. In sum, each book

- presents divergent, conflicting views on the problem under consideration;
- gives as many perspectives and dimensions on the problem as space permits;
- presents articles on a variety of reading levels, in order to appeal to students of many different ability levels;
- presents analytical as well as descriptive statements;
- deals with real people involved in situations of concern to them;
- includes questions which encourage discussion and thought of the various viewpoints expressed;
- includes activities to involve students to consider further the issues embedded in the problem.

CONTENTS

1 Introduction 1

2 Is There a Sexual Revolution? 5

3 What Is the 'New Morality'? 13

1. Some Thoughts on the Sexual Revolution 13
2. Anything Goes: Taboos in Twilight 17
3. Roman Holidays for Students 24
4. The Pill 27
5. A Reaction to the New Morality 31

4 What Sexual Attitudes Exist Today? 39

1. Teen-agers and Sex: A Student Report 39
2. What Do Teen-Agers Think About Changes in Morality? 46
3. Too Much Sex Too Soon? 51
4. The Population Explosion and Birth Control 56
5. A Different Religious Viewpoint 61
6. Opinions of the College Co-ed 65

5 How Are Culture and Sex Related? 73

1. Sex in Different Cultures 73
2. Morality and the English Teen-Ager 80

6 **What Influences Sexual Attitudes and Behavior? 88**

1. Today's Children and Sex 88
2. Today's Children and Sex: What Readers Think 95
3. Enlightenment or Demoralization? 99
4. Is Censorship an Answer? 102
5. Our Unlovable Sex Laws 105

Bibliography 113

1

Introduction

Dear Betty Lovelorn:

How does a teen-ager decide on the way to treat sex in America today? I am sixteen years old, a girl with pretty good looks and enough dates to keep busy. My problem is that I can't figure out how to act properly and still stay popular with boys. Some of my girlfriends say that you have to be free with boys if you expect to keep having dates, and some of the girls who are going steady are involved in heavy petting and other sex activities.

My parents have tried to teach me to be a "good" girl, but they don't seem to understand how it is in high school now. They get very upset if I stay out late on a date, and they want to know all about the boy and what happened. In church the Sunday school teacher talks a lot about morals and being a moral person, but she never talks about how to make the right decisions in sex. In school the teachers seem afraid to talk about sex and the special sex education class was girls only and spent all the time on hygiene and the biology of sex. The only place where I can talk about how to behave with boys is when I meet my friends in private.

Please tell me where I can find out about how to make the right decisions about sex.

B. R.

Dear Betty Lovelorn:

I am eighteen and engaged to be married soon. We have gone together for two years and are in love. Lately, my fiancé has been getting more insistent that we have premarital sex relations in order to make sure that we can get along after we're married. He says that it's better to find out before than to be unhappy afterward. I have resisted this idea because I was brought up to believe that sex should only be in marriage. Also, I am frightened that he would not be satisfied with me and that it might make us break up. Who is right in this argument?

C. M. F.

Dear Betty Lovelorn:

I have been reading the *Playboy* philosophy on sex and think that it is a cleaner and better way to look at sex and morals than what my parents and teachers have been saying. Why shouldn't boys and girls be allowed to practice free love if they want to and if it doesn't harm anyone else? Who says that virgins are better wives than nonvirgins? Why should a boy respect a girl who won't engage in love making when she may be just covering up her frigidity? If a boy and girl both desire sex and each other, why should they wait until marriage? Must sex be dirty? What right does anyone have to censor books and movies? If adults didn't think that sex is dirty, there would be no pornography. Why not let each person make up his own mind about what to read or see, how to behave, and what to think? Is there any crime in nudity? Why shouldn't homosexuals have their rights protected as long as they don't force others? Why are our laws so strict on sex? Isn't it a private affair?

I think the whole society would be better off if we quit acting like our Puritan ancestors, and become more relaxed about sex.

M. L. S.

Dear Betty Lovelorn:

Who do you think you are giving love advice to teen-agers? You have been writing a lovelorn column since my mother was a girl, and you haven't changed your advice in over thirty years. Don't you know that a sexual revolution has occurred? We don't wear bloomers and long skirts now. Kissing in public isn't a crime anymore. People can talk about sex in school, at home, at parties, and on the street. With the pill, we don't have to worry about pregnancy now. It is old-fashioned to have chaperones at dances and parties.

Teen-agers are more sophisticated now than ever before. We can't talk to our parents because we know at least as much about sex as they do. The stuffiness of their rules for being "nice" has made them not able to enjoy the natural kind of sex that the younger generation has. It is more wholesome to be open and frank about sex than to feel guilty or sinful about it.

Either change with the new generation or quit writing 1920 advice to today's teens.

F. M.

Sex, the three-letter word that stimulates strong opinions, emotional writing, and guilty feelings, has been a subject of poolroom talk, dormitory conversation, libraries of books, PTA meetings, medical conferences, lavatory walls, multi-million dollar movies, religious sermons, art works, public laws, and personal decisions. It is a powerful and controversial topic because it involves the values of each individual in a very personal way, and it also involves the basic value system of a society.

Sexual morality is both a personal and a social problem. Morality refers to a standard of what is right and good. All societies have some standards in regard to sexual behavior that have developed over a period of time. These standards change as they are influenced by prevailing ideas and actions of the society's members. Conversely, individual sexual standards tend to be modified by the attitudes expressed by friends, teachers, parents, writers, and others. The problem results from conflicts between the sexual standards of the society and the person, and changing ideas. A rapid change in standards is revolutionary; a more gradual change is evolutionary.

The problem for society is maintaining a stable code of sexual conduct based on agreed moral standards about such things as proper dress, the number of marriage partners permitted, acceptable literature and art, dating practices, and similar topics. The problem for individuals is establishing acceptable sexual behavior which accounts for social, personal, and biological needs.

There is a tendency for older persons to protect the ideals of the sexual morality under which they grew up, and for younger persons to question that morality. This book is concerned with the issues arising from conflicts in the sexual standards of a society and the behaviors of youth in contemporary life. Some of the questions that will be considered follow:

1. Are the changing patterns of sexual behavior in America revolutionary or evolutionary?
2. What do we mean by morality when it comes to sex?
3. What attitudes about sexual morality exist in America?
4. Is sexual freedom the same thing as promiscuity?
5. Who decides what kinds of sexual behavior are proper and what standards are to be used?
6. What cultural conditions influence sexual conduct?
7. What are some of the social, psychological, and personal implications of changes in attitudes and behaviors of youth in regard to:
   a. Premarital sexual relations?
   b. Illegitimate births?
   c. Birth control?
   d. Sex education?
   e. Pornography?

The readings in this book are not intended to provide you with answers to these questions. They do offer a variety of opinions and facts. In a topic as loaded with emotion as sex, it is sometimes very difficult to separate factual material from that which is primarily opinion. Both fact and opinion are important in the analysis of this social issue, because morality (a social and personal judgment of what is right and good) is largely based on opinions supported by whatever facts are available. Since sex has been mainly a personal and private matter, there are relatively few facts available.

This book presents issues regarding sexual attitudes and behaviors but does not cover the biological aspects of sex. An understanding of the biology of sex is equally important, and the bibliography provided at the end of the book offers suggestions for materials that deal with this information.

As you read the following selections try to separate fact from opinion, but use both to develop your own position on sexual morality in America.

2

Is There a Sexual Revolution?

Are the changes in American attitudes toward sex today revolutionary or evolutionary? What are some of the areas of change and stability in sexual affairs? How recent are the changes? How do teen-age sexual attitudes and behavior differ from those of previous times? This chapter presents a brief history of the development of sex norms in societies and the roles of older and younger generations in changing these norms.

The term prehistory simply means that period previous to written records. Written documents go back to about 4000 B.C. and provide information concerning the dominant social values in sexual conduct as well as other aspects of life. Archeologists have uncovered evidence about life in prehistoric times from wall drawings, carved statues, community structures, and the tools and implements used. From these artifacts archeologists reconstruct the kind of life which existed in prehistoric societies.

It is perhaps too obvious to state that sexual conduct is a part of the life style of any society. Man's need and ability to reproduce and his biological sex drive are universal, that is, they occur in every culture. The question is not whether sexual activities happened, but what kinds of social restrictions and freedoms were agreed to in early civilizations.

It is the socially accepted patterns, or norms, of sexual behavior that form the sexual morality of a society and determine any revolutionary or evolutionary change in these patterns. For example, if a society accepts the practice of monogamy (marriage with only one person at a time), it will establish codes that support monogamous marriage practices in that society. The codes may be formal laws as in the United States, or they may be informal sanctions which cause anyone who deviates to be ostracized or driven out of the society. The person who deviates from monogamy in such a society is often considered immoral. (His acts may also be illegal, but that is not a necessary condition for a judgment of immorality.)

If a younger generation, as a result of a variety of possible causes, begins to question the value of monogamy and can enlist sufficient popular support to make it a social issue, then a potential change in morality becomes evident. A sudden change to polygamy (a man's having more than one wife) or polyandry (a woman's having more than one husband) by a sizable number of people in a society would constitute a revolutionary change. A long-time movement to alter the marriage laws, with relatively minor changes at first and involving smaller proportions of the population, would be an evolutionary change.

PREHISTORIC SEXUAL MORALITY

It is generally believed that in prehistoric times the sexual habits of human beings led to customs related to both biological drives and group survival. The customs not only provided guidelines for the production of children, but also determined the arrangement by which males and females could protect, feed, and nurture their babies in some communal fashion. Differing groups of people developed somewhat different customs. Some groups had arrangements where one man and one woman lived together; she bore children and nursed them; he provided protection and support. Out of this pattern came taboos relating to sex conduct. These were, in turn, incorporated into laws or strong traditions as the society became more complex and regulation of behavior became socially important. The institution of the family, as it is known in many contemporary cultures, was formed when the earlier habits, customs, and rituals became the predominantly accepted way of life in a society.

Other groups developed different patterns of sexual relations, child-bearing, and child-rearing. One pattern was for sexual relations to be less directly tied to child-rearing. In this case the child became a responsibility of the whole group. Distinctions of motherhood and fatherhood, which were very important in the cultures that influenced the American system, were of little concern because the child was a community responsibility. The "family" consisted of a much larger group than simply mother-father-child. The customs which emerged from this pattern led to a system of sexual taboos, rituals, and morals different from the pattern of sexual morality prevalent in America today.

Presumably, the behavior of man was at first purely instinctive, similar to the behavior of animals. Food was fought over, and the stronger person won. A mate might also be fought over, and again the stronger man usually emerged the victor. Such animal instinctiveness was self-satisfying and self-preserving. Eventually, however, it became apparent that association with others, through common activities and group life, meant greater safety, more power, and better division of labor. In order for societies to exist and develop, many instinctive and emotional drives of individuals had to be controlled by the group. A society could not permit wanton killing or maiming of people without some controls. The same need for prohibitions apparently occurred with regard to sexual conduct.

Among primitive man sex had a superstitious basis. Rituals of puberty and fertility were related to beliefs about gods, good crops, and improvement of the society. Symbols representing the sex organs were used in crop planting and harvesting ceremonies, to decorate places of worship, and in rituals to protect and defend the society from human and spirit forces.

The attempts of early man to explain natural phenomena, such as thunder, earthquake, storm, and wind, developed into systems of belief which could be called religions. Early religious attitudes toward sex carried much of the same sex-symbolism of prior societies. Sexual organs are referred to with a degree of sacredness in early Jewish and Christian literature. Ancient Greek and Roman religion was permeated with sex. Art and architecture of the periods show the role of sex as a positive influence on society.

INFLUENCE OF CHRISTIANITY

As Christianity evolved, its most important concern was theological rather than sexual. Primary attention was given to the development of a systematic theory of Christian belief to serve as a basis for the religion. Sexual morality was of little importance outside of its relation to continuance of the species. For instance, there were no specific Christian marriage ceremonies during this period. Followers of Christianity were married in slightly altered civil ceremonies which had no particular theological interest. Marriage did not become a sacrament of the church until the Middle Ages.

There was, however, a strong ascetic attitude about life in general among prominent Christian leaders, and this attitude had increasing influence over sexual morality as Christianity expanded. Asceticism refers to the belief in and practice of self-denial for its moral and spiritual values. The ascetic view of life includes a rejection of worldly activities, including sex, and a rigid self-discipline. This view was strong in early Christianity and was important in establishing moral codes about sexual life that were very influential in later periods. The Puritans, a significant Christian group of early settlers in America, are considered to be modified ascetics.

The basic Christian tenet on sex was that it was only for procreation. The use of sex for personal gratification was considered sinful. Though sex could be accepted within marriage, sex outside of marriage was considered a mortal sin. Celibacy was believed to be spiritually superior to sex relations, and members of the clergy adopted a celibate state. Regarding sex as an evil also provided a religious basis for what had been the traditional lower status of women to men. Women were considered to be responsible for sin, as they reflected the role of Eve in the Biblical story of Eden.

The morality of a number of other human activities was also influenced by Christian tenets on sex. Homosexuality, masturbation, adultery, birth control, divorce, and other sex and marriage practices which deviated from lifetime, monogamous procreation or celibacy were labeled evil, sinful, and immoral.

PROTESTANTISM and SEX

The Catholic-Protestant split in Christian thought contributed to views on sexual morality. Protestant groups restricted sex to marriage, although some accepted the ideas that sex was not evil and that celibacy was not of a higher order than marriage. Protestantism held that adultery and fornication were sins, but sexual relations in marriage were not. Sex could be pleasurable as well as procreative; monogamy was the proper standard; some birth control could be exercised; and divorce and remarriage were permissible.

EARLY AMERICAN VIEWS

Puritan thought about sexual morality was the standard in early American history. Although there are records of groups in colonial America which permitted sexual conduct unacceptable to the Puritans, the major influence of what was moral came from Puritan beliefs. The main Puritan positions on sexual morality were based on the Calvinistic concept of the evilness of man. Man was considered essentially evil because he was the result of Adam's fall from grace in the Garden of Eden. Thus original sin—the sexual lust described by analogy in the story of Adam and Eve—committed mankind to a continuing search for salvation, normally through acceptance of church doctrine.

If man is considered basically evil, then society needs to establish rules and regulations to govern his conduct and control his outlets for evil. Early Puritan settlers in New England established rigid codes of behavior, including regulations that provided for severe punishment for children who were disrespectful, for people who did not attend church, or for anyone who spoke badly of the minister. Only those who were members of the church were permitted to vote. In this kind of society, sexual morality was also under rigid control by the elders and the church.

Children were taught of man's evilness very early. *The New England Primer,* widely used in colonial America for over 100 years, was the standard textbook and included strongly moralistic teachings to instruct the young in proper conduct. John Cotton and Cotton Mather, both of a famous Massachusetts family, wrote long treatises on how to bring up children. None of their suggestions, it should be noted, included permissiveness on the part of parents.

In later colonial times and continuing throughout the American Revolutionary Period, the move was toward political, social, and sexual liberalism. The most prominent shift was in the political area, leading to the overthrow of British colonial rule. There is some evidence, however, that there was a loosening of sexual morality from the more rigid Puritan position. Some authors have maintained that the upper class has never felt subject to moral codes, but has used such codes as a means of controlling lower-class behavior. Descriptions of European nobility and court life, and their apparent influence on segments of American society, would suggest that Puritan morality was not as prevalent in America during the 18th Century as it had been in the 17th.

It is important to note, however, that sexual morality and sexual behavior are not identical. Morality refers to the dominant set of values held in a society, and individuals or groups may behave in ways entirely opposite to those values. For example, one of the dominant American values is equalitarianism, yet we still have large portions of our society denied equal opportunities because of the behaviors and attitudes of some members of American society. We may consider premarital sex to be immoral, but some members of society engage in the practice. Or, we may change our morality to condone premarital sex between certain individuals, but that would not mean that all couples would behave in such a fashion.

VICTORIAN THOUGHT ON SEX

The family in Victorian times (from the middle of the 19th to the early 20th Century) was close-knit, relatively large, and generally of strict morality. Any sort of deviance from the public morality was chastised. Relatively rigid codes of conduct regulated proper dress, dancing, dating, and courtship. A person who flouted the codes was considered immoral, and his or her reputation was tainted in that community.

This is not to say that all persons behaved according to Victorian moral standards. Biographers of families of the time show that scandal was a part of many important families, but the families did their best to hide the stories of wayward relatives. In addition, among the younger generation, a rebellion against Victorian morality developed and culminated in the period known as the "Gay Nineties." The rugged individualism displayed in opening and settling the western frontiers during the 19th Century and the development of cities as focal points of American society tended to relax the rigidities of the sex attitudes of the time. Religion was no longer as powerful an influence in American life.

THE TWENTIETH CENTURY

A general loosening of strong parental control followed the Victorian Period, and the First World War stimulated the adventuresome nature of an American society that was becoming more international. Other countries had developed differing sex codes, but this was not widespread knowledge because of the Puritan-Victorian restrictions on sex education. As more and more Americans visited other countries, however, greater awareness of various sex attitudes developed.

In addition, the rapid changes brought about by the industrial revolution produced feelings of freedom in other aspects of the society (work, leisure, child-labor, and so forth), which influenced attitudes about sex. One of the most important movements in this regard was that of female emancipation. The attempts to achieve political, social, and economic equality for women in America brought changes in sexual attitudes. No longer were women to be viewed as property. They had been dragged off by mates in cave-man times; they had been slaves in some ancient civilizations; but now they were renouncing even the inferior status accorded them in early 20th Century America. Some women showed their new emancipation in the 1920's by defying the morals of the Victorian Period. The "flapper" girls with their short dresses, bobbed hair, free-style dancing, and open discussion of sex were a part of "Flaming Youth."

Other conditions contributed to the changes in sexual morality. The automobile removed courting from the front parlor and was under heavy fire from churches and various leaders of morality for its contribution to the changing sex habits of younger generations. The possibility of sex education was considered by many *avant garde* thinkers, and some schools experimented with special courses on sex.

Censorship of pornographic and obscene materials became more important to some members of society because of the increasing ease of production and the wider distribution of books and films. Some books which were readily available in Europe were not permitted into America. The ten-cent pulp magazines were decried in newspaper editorials and church pulpits as inducing immorality in the young. Movies that dealt with sex, or included sex in their stories, were criticized, and vigilante committees were established to act as censors.

SEXUAL MORALITY AND MODERN YOUTH

The morality derived from early Christian, Puritan, and Victorian thought continues to exert profound influence on contemporary America. The earlier traditions have, however, been modified by the Gay Nineties, Flaming Youth, and more currently, the "new morality." This latest term is difficult to specifically define, but refers to present changes in attitudes about sex in books and films, birth control, homosexuality, premarital relations, and the whole spectrum of social ideas about sex activities, particularly among the teen-age generation.

The following are excerpts from writings about youth and morality: [1]

> To many an observer this indifference of young people toward moral conditions is alarming, as it seems to indicate that we are acquiescing in what such observers call a moral and spiritual revolution whose consequences can hardly be other than subversive of the principles upon which manners and morals are based. Indeed, "revolution" is not the harshest word we hear. One critic prefers to term it "devolution." Another calls it "devilution" . . .
>
> The painful truth . . . is "not that standards have changed, but that there are no longer any standards at all" . . .
>
> The modern girl is an extremist. She dresses in the lightest and most flimsy of fabrics. Her dancing is often of the most passionate nature, and I believe the modern dance has done much to break down standards of morals. . . . The fellow of today, in most cases, will not go out with a girl for any period of time unless she permits him to caress her. . . .
>
> Neither sex has any illusions left regarding the other. . . .
>
> The seminudity of the girls who walk the streets and mingle with men in social gatherings raises the question whether the sense of modesty that once was a distinguishing mark of the pure woman is no longer a virtue, or whether the exposure of the person is meant to advertise an attitude that is inevitably suggestive.

Each of the above excerpts comes from a prominent person or some news media. They commonly express shock or dismay at alterations in the sex standards and behaviors of the younger generation. Is there a moral revolution? You will note in the footnote that all of the excerpts were published in a popular American magazine in 1921 and 1922. Could they have been published in 1965, 1968, or 1970?

The readings in this book are of more current vintage than 1921. They represent information and opinions about the questions of sex, morality, and contemporary teen-age behavior. Many adults today feel that teen-agers have lost their moral heritage, are too open about sex, appear to be promiscuous, and are destroying the moral fiber of this society. Many teen-agers feel that the restrictions on sex are old-fashioned

---

[1] Excerpts from "The Case Against the Younger Generation," *Literary Digest,* May 21, 1921, and "The Religious Press on Youthful Morals," *Literary Digest,* June 17, 1922.

and irrational, create guilt unnecessarily, and have nothing to do with the morality of individual conscience. On either side of the conflict are both adults and teen-agers. Many adults agree that greater sex freedom should be allowed, while many teen-agers support strong sex standards as a means of maintaining a stable society. What are your views?

What Do You Think?

1. How would you describe the present morality of teen-agers?
2. Has there been a revolution in sexual morality?
3. What comparisons can you draw between contemporary changes in sexual attitudes and changes in other aspects of American society?

3

What Is the 'New Morality'?

There is a difference of opinion today over whether the changes in sexual morality and conduct are revolutionary or evolutionary. Some have suggested that the changes move in a cycle, passing from strictness to looseness and then returning.

This chapter explores dimensions of the change through differing viewpoints. Is there anything new under the sun—even in sex?

1. SOME THOUGHTS ON THE SEXUAL REVOLUTION *

A writer, educator, and magazine editor, who has been an observer of American society and schools for a large part of the 20th Century, maintains that "sexual change" is cyclical. Does he convince you?

For as long as I can remember—and my memory for such things goes back into the Twenties—we have been hearing about something called a "sexual revolution." Undergraduates of the flapper era, who identified themselves with the "lost generation," dated the revolt from World War I. Students of the Thirties believed that it began with the Depression, which made marriage impossible for many young people, who consequently looked for other sexual outlets. Those of the Fifties thought the revolution was an aftermath of World War II and began when returning veterans encountered patriotic coeds. Today's undergraduates firmly believe that the revolt started about 1960, when they were in junior high, and that

* Reprinted from Paul Woodring, "Some Thoughts on the Sexual Revolution," *Saturday Review,* January 20, 1968, by permission of the publisher and author.

it is somehow related to both the threat of nuclear war and the invention of the Pill.

All these views reflect the innocence of youth, because neither sexual activity nor the discussion of it is as new as many students believe. In 1721, Harvard undergraduates formally debated the question: "Whether it be fornication to lye with one's sweetheart before marriage." It is unlikely that there has ever been a generation to whom sex was not a major interest or which did not include many individuals who violated the rules laid down for them by their elders. It might well be argued that the sexual revolt really began when Eve tempted Adam with the apple. It requires no great knowledge of history to know that the sexual mores are no more relaxed today than they have been at many times in man's long past, and that the loosening and tightening of the restrictions on sexual activity go in cycles of irregular length which are related to a wide variety of social forces and social changes.

The present trend toward a loosening of restraints dates roughly from the 1890's. It is not so much a revolution as a growing reaction against the restrictive sexual morality that has variously, and somewhat carelessly, been described as "Puritanical," "Victorian," or "middle-class." The trend was accelerated by the invention of the automobile, improvements in the techniques of birth control, the two world wars which took young men away from the restraining influences of their home communities, and the dislocation of families resulting from the move from farms and small towns to cities. Freer sexual activity was made to seem more necessary by the careless reading of Freud, and more normal—at least statistically—by the careful reading of Kinsey. It both gave rise to and fed upon the literature, motion pictures, and television programs of the twentieth century.

Early in this century, young people discovered that a date in a parked car could be something quite different from one in the front parlor with Mother hovering in the background. Those who first made this discovery, and who now are grandparents, are shocked to learn that students now have dates in dormitory rooms while the dean of women looks the other way. Perhaps the activities in either case do not differ greatly from those that took place on back porches or in lawn swings in the Nineties—research psychologists report that there are as many virgins among today's coeds in at least a few selected colleges as there were a generation ago. But most people are convinced that a larger proportion of today's adolescents now participate freely in what has always been the favorite sport of the human race.

Whatever the change in frequency or kind of activity—and no statistics on such a subject can be highly reliable—there has been a vast change in the kind of advice given to young people. A half-century ago, the books of intimate advice for boys and girls told readers that any sexual activity outside of marriage was sinful, and that premarital sex precluded the possibility of a happy marriage because no man respected a girl who allowed what then were called "liberties." Girls were told that anything more intimate than handholding aroused the baser passions in a man and could lead to no good end.

Some of the books read by teen-agers today still frown upon "heavy petting" and advise against premarital intercourse, but the reasons given usually are practical or psychological rather than ethical. Most of the authors agree that a modest degree of petting and fondling is a normal way of showing deep affection and that such preliminary activities are a necessary prelude to good marital adjustment. And every teen-ager has read at least one book by a psychiatrist, psychologist, or possibly a minister who sagely pontificates that, while caution is advisable and love is important, no activity involving two consenting adults is necessarily harmful or really sinful. Any reader who has reached the age of sixteen is certain that he is an adult and that the consent can be obtained —if necessary, with the aid of the book, which can be discussed on the next date.

Today's students, though they seem excessively eager to conform to the standard of the peer group if they can discover what it is, are not willing to accept an absolutist view of what is right and wrong. They have read enough history, anthropology, and literature to know that sexual morality differs from one culture to another and from one period to another within a culture. They have learned enough psychology to know that whether one will feel guilty about any kind of behavior depends on what he has been taught and what he has learned from his own experience. They know that pregnancy can now be prevented by anyone willing to plan ahead, and they have more confidence than may be justified in their ability to do the planning.

They are not inclined to accept the restrictions which adults attempt to place on their activities, because they are aware of a conspicuous gap between the publicly announced morality and the actual behavior of men and women. They know that many "respectable" adults—including, quite possibly, their own parents—have at times violated the conventions and seem to be none the worse for it. They are convinced that the older generation hypocritically gives lip service to a code in which it does not really believe and which it does not always follow. And they are contemptuous of hypocrisy.

The dilemma faced by young people is clear enough. Human males reach their period of greatest sexual vigor and desire at a time prior to marriage, when the doors to socially approved sexual activity are closed to them. But these doors, which have never been successfully locked and barred, have now been set aside by a more permissive society. The dilemma faced by girls, though different, is no less perplexing. Though some girls have strong sexual urges, more of them are motivated more by the desire to be popular with boys or by the desire to please one particular boy. They do not want to be thought old-fashioned, moralistic, or "square." When they ask their elders "What are the permissible limits?" the usual answer is, "It all depends." Consequently, they are not likely to conclude that all sexual activity must be avoided until marriage.

In the absence of an effective and accepted code, each boy and girl must decide for himself where to draw the line. This places an enormous strain on each individual because, as Richard Hettlinger reminds us in *Living with Sex: The Student's Dilemma,* "There is no field of human activity in which it is so easy to deceive oneself and to be convinced by arguments which are in fact nothing but rationalizations of clamant desires." A young man or woman needs all the advice he can get from older people whose desires presumably have cooled a bit and who can take a longer view. But, being young, he is not likely to take it.

A new code of sexual behavior—one that can be accepted by young people—clearly is needed. In our pluralistic society, a code that is to be effective must be acceptable to Catholics, Jews, and Protestants of many denominations, as well as to the agnostics and atheists who are found in substantial numbers on most campuses, because all these groups exchange dates. The fact that this seems a large order probably explains why a new morality has been so slow to emerge; but, unless it does, we are faced with the prospect of moral chaos, because the older sexual morality, based as it was on a combination of religion, tradition, and fear of pregnancy and disease, is no longer effective with the younger generation.

The new code must be consistent with the knowledge now available from psychology, sociology, anthropology, and biology. It must be based on a clear recognition of the fact that most of the educated and enlightened people living today, whether young or old, look upon sexual desire as biologically, socially, and psychologically normal rather than as something evil, dirty, and shameful. And it must reflect the fact that the double standard is no longer acceptable to educated people, nor is the view that desire to produce offspring is the only legitimate motivation for sexual activities.

Unless a new code emerges, we are likely to see a continued relaxation of standards, a growing contempt for the traditions and laws governing sexual activities, and still more confusion on the part of young people as to what is and is not acceptable and moral. If our culture takes a downward trend, historians and archaeologists of the future who examine the remnants probably will conclude that a decline of sexual morality was a major cause of the deterioration. But if our culture continues to survive and flourish despite a greater degree of sexual freedom, tomorrow's historians may call attention to the fact that sexual freedom has been a characteristic of many of the greatest periods of human achievement. And they will find many examples to cite.

What Do You Think?

1. Would you agree that a "new code of sexual behavior" is needed, as this writer suggests?
2. Why is it difficult for so many young people to take advice on sexual (or other) matters from their elders?

2. ANYTHING GOES: TABOOS IN TWILIGHT *

A popular magazine recently reviewed the nature of the "new morality" and presented this judgment.

The old taboos are dead or dying. A new, more permissive society is taking shape. Its outlines are etched most prominently in the arts—in the increasing nudity and frankness of today's films, in the blunt, often obscene language seemingly endemic in American novels and plays, in the candid lyrics of pop songs and the undress of the avant-garde ballet, in erotic art and television talk shows, in freer fashions and franker advertising. And, behind this expanding permissiveness in the arts stands a society in transition, a society that has lost its consensus on such crucial issues as premarital sex and clerical celibacy, marriage, birth control and sex education; a society that cannot agree on standards of conduct, language and manners, on what can be seen and heard.

While artists and writers hail this new candor as a release from an era of Victorian repression and hypocrisy, many Americans are bewildered and concerned about the swiftness with which all the old restraints are losing their force. Mores are changing so fast, in fact, that the biting, bitchy language of "Who's Afraid of Virginia Woolf?" which caused Hollywood to rewrite its Production Code only eighteen months ago, today sounds surprisingly tame. " 'Virginia Woolf' is vanilla compared to the film version of 'Ulysses,' " says Jack Valenti, president of the Motion Picture Association of America, who has helped to modernize a Hollywood Production Code that is already obsolete. "Films can't live in a vacuum. They relate to the temper of the times, the postures of today."

These new postures alarm many citizens, psychologists and social thinkers who see in this rapid destruction of taboos a dangerous swing toward irresponsible hedonism and, ultimately, social decay. "It is the inevitable mark of decadence in our society," says British social commentator Malcolm Muggeridge. "As our vitality ebbs, people reach out for vicarious excitement, like the current sex mania in pop songs and the

* Excerpted from *Newsweek,* November 13, 1967. Reprinted by permission, *Newsweek.*

popular press. At the decline and fall of the Roman Empire, the works of Sappho, Catullus and Ovid were celebrated. There is an analogy in that for us."

There are others, however, who reject the notion that the new permissiveness is a sign of moral collapse. "We are just beginning to discover what morality is all about," says theater critic Kenneth Tynan. "It is concerned with how we behave toward each other, not how much of our bodies we happen to display. There will be no return to the horse and buggy or to full-length skirts."

CHANGE

Indeed, the revolution in manners and morals that has produced a climate of candor is very real and unlikely to reverse itself. "We're going to have to live with a degree of freedom much greater than anything we've known in the past," says Father Walter J. Ong, the brilliant Jesuit theologian and author of "The Presence of the Word." "Man can't just say anything goes and hope to get by. We're going to have to employ our minds and morals in determining that some things go and other things don't. We're going to have to constantly reassess the situation because the situation will always be changing." . . .

"We're living in a Babylonian society perhaps more Babylonian than Babylon itself," says historian and columnist Max Lerner. "It's what's called a late sensate period. The emphasis in our society today is on the senses and the release of the sensual. All the old codes have been broken down."

This new freedom of expression is unlikely to reverse itself because the forces that have produced it are a permanent and irresistible part of modern life. The history of the arts itself has been a constant assault on forms and conventions to get at the essence of man and explore the deepest regions of his mind, spirit—and body. . . .

"What was once the realm of private knowledge has become public knowledge," says Father John M. Culkin, director of communications at Fordham and a disciple of media-master Marshall McLuhan. "Perhaps there's too much honesty but there's no doubt that these things have become part of the public domain." And this articulation of the inner self and man's own sexuality is not limited to artists alone. Today, the concepts and language pioneered by Freud are openly used in the discussion of sexual problems. "Freud showed us we were not alone," says Father Ong. "We feel so close to one another that nobody has any secrets any more."

This common admission of sexuality ultimately finds expression in franker sex-education courses in the Anaheim, California, and Evanston, Illinois, school systems, in which grade-school children are encouraged to bring the whispered words of the playground into the classroom for open discussion. It permits the creation of special high schools for pregnant girls in San Francisco and New York. It enables both clerics and laymen within the Roman Catholic Church to challenge pastoral policy on celibacy and birth control. It even permits the manufacture of baby-boy dolls equipped with sex organs.

APPETITES

The climate of candor in America today is not, however, simply a matter of art and expression pushing forward to the applause of an increasingly tolerant public. There have always been writers like Havelock Ellis and D. H. Lawrence willing to talk frankly and an audience willing to listen. But, until recently, agencies of moral order like the church, the government, the family and the community have dictated what can and cannot be expressed in public. Since World War II, in America, however, these institutions have simply been overrun by the demands of a mass society that wants to see and hear everything.

Nowhere has this process been more graphically dramatized than in the erosion of film censorship. In the 1930's fear of government regulation drove Hollywood to create its own Production Code, which forbade a husband and wife to be shown in the same bed and banned the word buzzard because it sounded too much like bastard. The Roman Catholic Church also controlled film content through its Legion of Decency, whose "C" or "condemned" rating could bar a movie from hundreds of theaters fearful of local boycott.

After the second world war, however, both code and church censorship started to crack. In 1946, Howard Hughes released "The Outlaw" in the face of a "C" rating and culled a fortune on the strength of Jane Russell's titanic cleavage. Seven years later, when both the Legion and Hollywood refused to sanction "The Moon is Blue" because of the word "virgin," producer Otto Preminger released it anyway and was amply reimbursed by the public. Again, in 1956, Preminger defied the code and its taboo on dope addiction when he released "The Man With the Golden Arm."

FEEBLE

Since then, the code has been revised twice, and the Legion of Decency has changed its name to the National Catholic Office for Motion Pictures and has liberalized its judgments. But the power of both agencies is now feeble. . . . "As far as I'm concerned the public makes up its own mind," says the 73-year-old chief executor of the Production Code, Geoffrey Shurlock. "America has in time grown up to accept sex. All the taboos are beginning to break down, which is probably the most healthy thing that could happen." Adds Fordham's Father Culkin: "Now the media goes directly to the public. The moralizers got so out of touch, they shouted for so long, that after a while nobody listened."

The courts, the last official restraining arm of society, have developed in recent cases such fluid guidelines for obscenity that local police agencies can seize and prosecute only those films and books that are "utterly without socially redeeming value." "Censorship of films and books has become simply a matter of taste," says veteran lawyer Ephraim London, an expert on censorship who has argued a number of key cases before the Supreme Court. "Today there's absolutely nothing you can't show or write about if it's done in good taste, absolutely nothing. If the courts judge something obscene, they are in effect making an aesthetic rather than a moral judgment. If the censorship rules of 1950 were in effect today, two out of every three films shown now would be banned." Even many of the tasteless hard-core paperbacks which could, under the law, be seized are more often than not ignored by district attorneys who feel no real pressure to do so from the community.

METAPHOR

The shattering of taboos on language, fashion and manners generally is part of a larger disintegration of moral consensus in America. Vast numbers of Americans distrust their government. Catholics in increasing numbers simply ignore the church ban on birth control. The family has changed from a breeding ground of common values into a battleground of generations. These dislocations have moved many writers to reach for the strongest language in their arsenal to capture the chaos of their time. "We're in a time that's divorced from the past," says novelist Norman Mailer. "There's utterly no tradition anymore. It's a time when our nervous systems are being remade. There's an extraordinary amount of obscenity around—and it's in my new book. I had to write it that way despite the fact that I hate to add to all that obscenity." But such language, insists Mailer, "is the only metaphor to express the situation that produces Vietnam." . . .

Things have changed radically since Mailer, in "The Naked and the Dead," had to invent the word "fug" to evoke the raw language of the American soldier in World War II. Today Mailer, Hubert Selby, and a whole school of new young novelists use obscenity not merely as an imitation of street speech but as an antidote to their own outrage and frustration at what they feel is the increasing dehumanization of the high-technology industrial state. "The real choice we have is not between dirty and not dirty," says Mailer. "It is between the creative artist, with his more or less corrupt soul, explaining life with his instinctive and curious gift for language, and the scientist, with his more or less corrupt soul, explaining life with his lenses, galvanometers and probes."

MAMMAL

Obscenity and nudity and eroticism, then, have become prime weapons for the artist as humanizer. He uses them to remind man that, amidst his electrical appliances and armaments and credit cards and daily costumes, he remains Homo sapiens. "Why don't we stop pretending that we're not mammals and that we don't do the things mammals do?" asks poet-playwright Michael McClure, author of "The Beard." "There's nothing new about my play. It could have been done 2,000 years ago." Man as mammal, sexual, innocent, is the theme of today's erotic painters who use nudity to affirm life.

Inevitably, freedom of expression in an open society is as accessible to the smutmaster as to the serious artist. If the new candor has strengthened the writing of America's best novelists, it has merely polluted the pulp literature that sells to millions. Many best sellers simply pander perversions and profanity for profit. "These books aren't written, they're manufactured by formula," says Bennett Cerf, head of Random House and a pioneer in the publication of "Ulysses." "They set up a list of perversions and throw them in at 30-page intervals."

SMUT

. . . Twenty-three separate bills on obscenity [were] introduced into the 90th Congress. One, which establishes a Presidential commission on obscenity and pornography, passed this year [1967] after eight years of effort by South Dakota's Sen. Karl Mundt. The commission, to be composed of eighteen citizens appointed by the President, will spend up to $75 a day studying dirty books, working out a fresh definition of pornography and investigating the sale and distribution of smut with a view to proposing new legislation for its control. The commission has stirred very little enthusiasm in Washington. Most officials agree with the U. S. Post Office's general counsel Timothy May. "Sex is troubling for society, but government ought to stay out of it," he says, "unless there is widespread licentiousness which becomes harmful. The government is not here to enforce the Ten Commandments, and the wants of society are generally twenty years ahead of government."

Even the most powerful agent of moral restraint, the Catholic Church, has been struggling not to suppress the new candor but to develop a more flexible attitude itself in an effort to remain relevant within the permissive society. While conservative clerics in Rome, like Cardinal Alfredo Ottaviani, deplore the relaxation of mores in the West, more "progressive" prelates urge a liberalization of the traditional Catholic position on sex and sin. "A lot of religious people realize that the Carrie Nation approach to obscenity is no longer the style of our life," says Father John Reedy, editor of Ave Maria Magazine, one of a number of Catholic journals pressing for change. "Today's attitude is to appeal to the individual as an adult."

In fact, much of the new candor is coming from dissident Catholics themselves, among them the growing number of priests who are openly attacking the church policy on celibacy. One, James Kavanaugh, author of "A Modern Priest Looks at his Outdated Church," has left the church, but his attacks continue. "The church cannot subdivide the moral law into tiny absolutes," he says. "It cannot make God into a crotchety old lady with frayed nerves. The church's distorted image of man's weakness and inclination to sin prevents it from serving the people." "Religion has been used to cover up things," comments Lutheran theologian Martin L. Marty. "Some churchmen have simply said 'We are sick and tired of it.' They'll grab all kinds of instruments to change it—the most evocative tools at hand, both literary and linguistic."

SHAPE

In any case, no action, by either church or state, is likely to impede the advance of the permissive society. Already rumbles from other Western countries suggest the shape of things to come in America. Recently, in Holland, a nude girl appeared on Dutch national television with only a newspaper occasionally between her and the camera; there was no great public outcry. . . . And French director Roger Vadim . . . in "Barbarella" presents not only his wife, Jane Fonda, in the nude, but a glimpse of the year 40,000 in which, as he explains it, "there are no taboos on sex, eroticism or nudity, no sin in nudity or the sex act."

Vadim's vision of the earth as a great pleasure dome is as speculative as anyone else's. But it does raise the crucial question of where the new permissiveness is leading, whether the breakdown of the old order is going to lead to some new moral system or whether it is simply going to lead to the progressive discarding of all social restraint. Some artists and critics feel it is not going to lead anywhere, that it is simply one more swing in the pendulum of history between Dionysian [1] and Apollonian [2] styles of behavior. "I would expect the pendulum to swing back," says British director Tony Richardson. "Another historical movement will occur, some major cataclysm, and society will need heroics, more codes, ideals. All victories are limited; they are never total. Just when you think you have advanced for all time, you find you are mistaken."

Architect and cosmic thinker Buckminster Fuller believes the pendulum is swinging back already—not the pendulum of history, but of evolution. As Fuller sees it, man's role as a procreator in an advanced society diminishes as fewer and fewer offspring are needed to ensure the survival of the species. "In the days of baby-making," he says, "the

---

[1] Sensuous and frenzied in character. Relating to the Greek god Dionysus, the god of wine.

[2] Harmonious and balanced in character. Relating to the Greek god Apollo, the god of sunlight, music, and poetry.

forbidden areas of the body were kept secret and promising in order to make us look forward to getting into bed. Once we start exposing ourselves as we're doing, sex gets to be a bore. The sexes themselves start to blur, and homosexuality increases, which also cuts down babies. Nature is putting on the brakes and man is unconsciously following. This is really an anti-erotic and anti-sexual trend."

Most social thinkers, however, are unwilling to accept the dictates either of history or evolution, believing that man still exerts a crucial control over the shape of his future. They see the tumbling of the old codes not as the beginning of a moral decline, but as the beginning of a search for new values. If society does collapse in a hedonistic frenzy, it will be because this search has failed. "I think it's good to have an expressive, free and imaginative society," says Max Lerner, "as long as you recognize some limits. These limits don't have to be puritanical. Without limits, our society can become as hedonistic as the world of the Marquis de Sade—going toward the most sadistic and primitive drives in the human being. It's not enough to break things down. Such a trend is not ultimately satisfying in itself. New values must be found and I believe young people are trying to find these values. That's where I place my hope."

PRUDERY

It is impossible to know, right now, what new values will rise from the rubble of the old dispensations. Obviously, the emergence from prudery and hypocrisy imposes new responsibilities as it opens up new possibilities. Surely the lesson has been learned a thousand times that freedom is what one makes of it. Father Ong is guardedly optimistic. "The new permissiveness," he says, "lends us access at last to areas that were so heavily guarded and repressed that they interfered with our understanding of one another. This can be a very humanizing thing."

The permissive society, then, is an inevitable stage in a time of transition, a collective experiment in which spring up cheek by jowl the honest movies and the trashy ones, the vulgar books and the serious, the tough-minded plays and the titillating—all tolerated with an implicit faith that the new freedom will ultimately humanize and improve rather than corrupt. The breakdown of the traditional consensus has broadened the options available to each individual as to how he conducts his life. What he does with this freedom is another matter, and so far confusion and anxiety have characterized the new moral atmosphere.

PRESSURE

In this situation, serious artists need all the freedom they can get to express the roots of disorder and the possibilities for order. And with that freedom goes a tremendous responsibility. "Individuals are going to have to stiffen their own moral principles," says Father Ong. "They're going to live under a great deal of pressure. They won't be able to reverse this permissive trend but they can point out rational limits. They are going to have to speak up in a pluralistic society."

Whether the new freedom produces good or ill depends on man himself. "Is man essentially a hedonistic, pleasure-loving, self-indulgent type?" asks theologian Martin Marty. "Or is he essentially a purposeful, work-oriented, self-denying creature? We simply don't know." What happens in the permissive society will go a long way toward telling us.

What Do You Think?

1. Would you agree that "all the taboos are beginning to break down" in America? What evidence can you cite to support or refute this idea?
2. Can laws stop obscenity? Why or why not?
3. What does the saying "freedom is what one makes of it" mean? What, if anything, does it have to do with sexual morality?"

3. ROMAN HOLIDAYS FOR STUDENTS *

The "new morality" has been debated for a considerable time. Russell Kirk, in the following essay, suggests that the newness in morality today is really the "old immorality" of earlier times. He draws similarities between lack of morality in sexual life and lack of moral concern in other human activities.

The popular magazines are full, nowadays, of lurid accounts of "sexual orgies" among college students. Though one may discount somewhat the reports of societies on the campus for "sexual freedom," it remains true that a great deal of silliness about the purpose and pleasures of sexual relationship prevails today among students—and professors also, too often.

An able young professor as a good private university sends the following enlightening comments:

> I must confess that popular attitudes regarding sex have changed so drastically just in my lifetime that I find myself unable to adjust to, let alone accept these sudden innovations—or, as you say, this reversion to the "Old Immorality." At a student discussion of such topics that I attended recently, along with other members of the

---

* From Russell Kirk, *National Review,* May 16, 1966.

faculty, the girls left me absolutely flabbergasted. They talked about "sleeping with our boy friends," and were troubled by the fact that they were uncertain as to whether they intended to marry them. Many complained about "antiquated regulations" and "outmoded Puritan codes" which made it impossible for some and difficult for all to obtain contraceptives—thus "thwarting the full development of our personalities."

All seemed to favor abortion, which in my ancient household was regarded as murder. I had the impression that I was sitting in on a rehearsal for Brave New World, to be put on by the local drama club. Being a minority of one, I tended to swallow my protest, and was too busy catching my breath to utter a word. I continue to walk as if I were in a dream.

My friend's impressions of the decay of normative consciousness, among students, in this realm, are confirmed by many observers of the campus of this decade. Take this passage from Mr. John Keats' admirable book *The Sheepskin Psychosis:*

The dominant student and faculty opinion is that each student has the right to decide whether to engage in sexual intercourse, and that if a boy and girl are in love, they ought to go to bed together. On the other hand, the overwhelming opinion of college deans and psychiatrists is that most undergraduates are emotionally unready for coitus, and that they should therefore not engage in it.

But college authorities, their own apprehension of normality enfeebled by a generation of American permissivism, often do little to discourage actions which they consider mistaken and mischievous. A few days ago, this commentator conversed with a tolerant and rather witty widow who has become a housemother to a fraternity at a large Midwestern state university. She finds it difficult to maintain even the outward decencies in the house which she is supposed to chaperone; and, sub rosa, the college authorities tell her to absent herself from the fraternity house when there approaches any prospect of general impropriety. Were she to lodge a complaint in official quarters, founded upon charges against individual students, the college authorities simply would close the fraternity house, obliterating guilty and innocent at one blow, to preserve the college's "public image."

"PEER GROUP" ARBITERS

Such abdication of responsibility by college administrators—and, commonly by students' parents—delivers the average collegian to the domination of their "peer group" arbiters of taste and morality. (Most human beings always have acquired their moral habits from emulation and deference; and, nature abhorring a vacuum, if students have no strong good personalities to emulate, they must defer to strong corrupt personalities.) Thus, in dormitories or fraternities, often the general attitude toward sexual conduct is determined by the more reckless, unscrupulous, and "worldly" students. In the phrase of Yeats,

> The best lack all conviction, while the worst
> Are full of passionate intensity.

The fraternity housemother whom I mention above remarked to me that of the 35 men in her house, about five are genuine students; the rest have come to college for the fun and games, or to escape the draft, or for lack of anything better to do. Most of them have plenty of money to spend, and few serious lessons to prepare, and inadequate previous instruction from their parents. Idle and bored, is it any wonder they turn to sexual diversion, so readily available? When the campus has become principally a carnival, it is only a short remove from the bawdy-house.

JADED GRADS?

Mere exhortation will not remedy this folly. "The girls are worse than the boys at the 'mattress parties,' " my friend the housemother told me. With us, at the moment, was a youngish professor who once was a military intelligence officer and knows much of the world's ways. "How jaded those girls will be, when they graduate!" he murmured. "Life will seem to have no future."

Colleges exist primarily to make possible academic leisure. But that leisure is not supposed to be idleness, and it is supposed to be academic rather than sybaritic.[1] When colleges have lost any clear apprehension of their ethical end (which is attained through an intellectual means); when the professors have sunk into a disintegrated Liberalism that teaches merely "do as you will"; when the students, or most of them, have no genuine intellectual interests or aspirations—why, need we be surprised that Behemoth State University (formerly Dismal Swamp Teachers College) slides mindlessly into the "orgie-porgie" of Brave New World.

What Do You Think?

1. What is the relation among morality, immorality, and amorality?
2. How do changes in sexual morality reflect or change morality in other human affairs like crime, respect, work relations, race, etc.?

---

[1]Luxuriously sensual. Derived from Sybaris, an ancient city notorious for its inhabitants' wealth and love of pleasure.

4. THE PILL *

None of the various methods of birth control used in the past seems to have had the social impact of the oral contraceptive. Sociologists, educators, and churchmen are concerned about the questions it raises. In what ways might "the pill" affect American culture?

An era of vast change in sexual morality now is developing in America.

Fear is being expressed that the nation may be heading into a time of "sexual anarchy."

Just six years ago the birth-control pill came onto the market. Today—

· College girls everywhere are talking about the pill, and many are using it. The pill is turning up in high schools, too.

· Tens of thousands of Roman Catholic couples are turning to the pill as a means of practicing birth control.

These and other trends are expected to accelerate in times just ahead as laboratories perfect the long-term "contraceptive shot" and the "retroactive" pill which wards off pregnancy even if taken after sexual intercourse.

Result: Widespread concern is developing about the impact of the pill on morality.

Being asked are these questions: With birth control now so easy and effective, is the last vestige of sexual restraint to go out the window?

Will mating become casual and random—as among animals?

Recently, John Alexander, general director of the Inter-Varsity Christian Fellowship, which has its headquarters in Chicago, said:

"I think it is certain that the pill will tear down the barriers for more than a few young people hitherto restrained by fear of pregnancy—and this will be even more true when the 'retroactive' pill comes on the market.

"I am very much afraid that sexual anarchy could develop."

Disquiet is voiced even by an official of Planned Parenthood-World Population, which actively promotes birth control. Dr. Donald B. Strauss said:

"The two great supports of sexual morality in the past—fear of disease and fear of pregnancy—have now, happily, been largely removed . . .

"This, I submit, leaves our generation of parents with a problem that largely remains unsolved."

---

* Excerpted from *U. S. News & World Report,* July 11, 1966. Copyright © 1966 U. S. News and World Report, Inc.

EARLY PROMISCUITY

The dimensions of that problem are being outlined daily by signs of growing sexual promiscuity among America's young.

The Connecticut State department of health recently estimated that one 13-year-old girl out of every 6 in that State will become pregnant, out of wedlock, before she is 20.

Almost countless incidents have been reported, across the U. S., of teen-age girls in high schools carrying birth-control pills.

In some cases, these have been supplied by their parents.

"Sex clubs" at high schools are reported from time to time.

On the East Coast, high-school girls of the middle- and upper-income classes join a steady traffic reported among college girls who fly to Puerto Rico for legalized abortions.

Recently a freshman at one of the East's most exclusive girls' colleges told her parents that, when a group in her class visited an Ivy League university as week-end guests, her classmates stayed the night at motels with boys—some of whom they had never seen before and might never see again.

Such occurrences, she said, were commonplace and there were eight or nine pregnancies in her class during the past academic year. Girls declining to engage in sex relations were regarded as "squares," she said.

A DIFFERENT OUTLOOK

Seen as playing an important role in this form of "sexual anarchy" among youngsters is a new attitude toward morality. An official at Mills College in Oakland, Calif., reported that "there is less talk than there used to be about 'right or wrong'—the question today is more, 'Is the individual making a wise decision for her future?' " . . .

"When you talk to the girls today, you're talking in a whole new world. They know how to get the pill. They think a girl is a fool not to use it if—it's a big 'if'—she is seriously in love. Promiscuity is still frowned upon; but it's not equated with morals. It's a matter of personal pride."

Most educators appear to agree with an official of Ohio State University who described the vast majority of students as "nice, normal young people" but admitted that "this whole area of sexual morals is like an iceberg—some of it is visible but the extent of the submerged part is unknown."

One thing is clear: The pill, itself, now is becoming a major topic of conversation among students, and among faculty members, too, on nearly all the nation's campuses.

"I would rather be asked for the pills than for an abortion," this physician was quoted as saying.

In the medical profession, however, some uneasiness is beginning to be felt on the problem. It is being pointed out by some physicians that a doctor could be sued by a girl's parents—or charged with contributing to the delinquency of a minor—if he prescribes the pill without her parents' consent.

As a result, some physicians are prescribing pills for unmarried girls only on a restricted basis. For example, a Washington, D. C., gynecologist said:

"If a young woman over 18 years old came in and told me that she wanted a prescription because she was getting married, I would be inclined to give it to her. But, of course, I'd have no way of knowing for sure that she really was getting married."

Still other physicians are refusing prescriptions to unmarried girls on any basis. In San Francisco, one said:

"I don't like to give pills to a girl without her parents' consent, although I do know that girls can get them freely and are doing so. Some girls get a big supply and pass them around. Some deterrent is needed, and having to tell their parents first is a deterrent."

STUDENT ACTION

Today, a movement appears to be developing among students to force colleges to make pills available to them at college health clinics.

At the University of Texas, a candidate for president of the student body proposed that the pill be dispensed at the student health center. He lost the election, but it was agreed that he had developed a "popular issue."

At Stanford University, students voted more than 2 to 1 in favor of authorities' making contraceptives available to students on an "individual basis," as once was the case. The practice was stopped in 1962 because of complaints from parents, religious groups and alumni. The university administration has indicated that it has no intention of resuming the practice.

Much of the student demand is found to center in metropolitan areas, where, it is pointed out, official policy now is to dispense the pill freely to growing numbers of welfare clients, including many with records of sexual promiscuity.

CHANGING ATTITUDES

Until recently church pressure was a curb on private, as well as public, clinics for birth control among the poor.

Today, however, welfare administrators everywhere are turning to the pill as a means of keeping women from producing large broods, many illegitimate, to be supported by the public treasury.

New York, Chicago and Washington, D. C., at first limited birth-control services among the poor to married women. Now unmarried women, too, are getting the pill in those cities.

A number of officials and clergymen are voicing concern over this trend. Unchecked, they say, it could lead to official endorsement of the idea that sexual promiscuity is acceptable as long as pregnancy does not result. The Rev. Dexter L. Hanley, S. J., of Georgetown University's law school, told a Senate subcommittee on May 10:

"There are those who sincerely feel that the distribution of information and supplies to the unmarried will encourage promiscuity and a breakdown of public morality . . . If contraceptive advice is to be distributed to the unmarried, two things will be necessary . . . firstly, adequate counseling and increased attention to family values . . . secondly, doctors and counselors will have to be able to exercise discretion."

Still another moral dilemma is arising from use of the pill—this one involving Roman Catholic married couples.

Recently a Government-financed study showed that 21 per cent of Catholic wives under the age of 45 have used, or are using, birth-control pills despite the Church's ban on all unapproved means of family planning.

The comparable figure for Protestant wives was 29 per cent.

A number of Catholic clergymen have held the pill to be morally acceptable—not an "unnatural" process as the Church has held earlier contraceptives to be.

Dr. John Rock, a leading Catholic layman and one of the pioneers of the birth-control pill, said:

"There have been several statements made by authoritative theologians that the method by which the pill works is not clearly against nature, and that there is justification for use of the pill by those who, in all conscience, feel they should practice family planning by this means. . . .

DECISION FOR THE FUTURE

Dr. Rock and other Catholics make it clear, however, that all judgment must be reserved on the "retroactive pill" or the long-lasting "contraceptive shot" when these products appear on the market. Their view is that if either acts as an "abortive agent," it must be regarded as against the rule of nature, hence banned for use by Catholics.

These devices of the future, other clergymen are saying, are likely to multiply the moral dangers that are now arising as a result of the pill in its present form. . . .

WHAT SOCIOLOGISTS THINK

Sociologists point out that the pill, itself, is only one element in the danger of moral anarchy.

Dr. Mary S. Calderone, executive director of the Sex Information and Education Council of the U. S., said:

"Society provides young people with far too many examples of sex irresponsibly used. High-school kids see sex used as a commercial come-on, as an end in itself, presented to them. If the pill hadn't come along, we would be excited about whatever methods were being used."

Even so, the pill is becoming a major factor in the problem. Six million American women are using it. This sudden and overwhelming popularity has caused a few physicians to caution that physical effects over the long run are not thoroughly known. But neither these reservations nor the moral issues are dimming the enthusiasm felt by many Americans. One social worker said:

"The pill is so clean and simple, and sure, that everybody who hears about it wants it. And I tell everybody about it."

Crisis ahead? Less enthusiastic are many Americans who feel that the pill is making moral choices much more difficult for a lot of people, and could precipitate a crisis in sexual morality.

Recently the Right Rev. Richard S. Emrich, Episcopal Bishop of Michigan, said:

"The existence of the pill opens up dangerous possibilities . . . It provides an invitation to premarital sex. There must be limitations and restrictions on the use of sex if we are to remain a civilized people."

What Do You Think?

1. Is the use of the pill moral?
2. May "sexual anarchy" be the result of the new morality?
3. What are the religious problems associated with birth control by pills?
4. How obtainable should contraceptive devices be?

5. A REACTION TO THE NEW MORALITY *

Here is a response to the "revolutionary," "evolutionary," or "devolutionary" changes in sex in America. The remarks which follow were excerpted from the foreword to a book titled The Great Sex Swindle. *Does the title seem appropriate?*

---

* From "Foreword" by O. Hobart Mowrer to John W. Drakeford, *The Great Sex Swindle,* Nashville, Tenn.: Broadman Press, 1966. Reprinted by permission.

Some five years ago an editor of one of our more dignified women's magazines said to me: "The younger people on our editorial staff are now in control, and they are insisting that everything we publish, fiction and nonfiction alike, be 'permissive.' Anything that tries to hold up the standards of traditional morality they regard not only as having poor reader appeal but as a kind of evil in its own right." The speaker was a refined, gentle woman in her middle sixties who, without bitterness or self-pity, made it clear that her heart was no longer in her work. And one had the feeling that she represented a type of person who was not only vanishing from the publishing business but also from our society at large.

This woman, if she happened to see it, would have taken wry satisfaction in a piece which appeared a few months ago in the "Books" section of *Time* magazine. The author was simultaneously reviewing two or three new novels that were freighted with the kind of sexuality which, in literary circles, is today regarded as sophisticated—and salable. But the reviewer was obviously bored, and his whole piece was a poorly concealed, elaborate yawn.

The two incidents to which I have just alluded are, of course, in themselves trivial; but I believe they bracket a development of considerable significance. During the period in question, *Time, Newsweek, Life, Look,* and several other nationally important periodicals have published feature stories on the moral crisis of our time, particularly in the realms of sex, business, and government; and all of these articles have sounded a note of concern and apprehension. It would thus appear that we have at last touched bottom as far as the cult of permissiveness is concerned and are in the process of trying to recover an orderly way of life, or else find the basis for some sort of new morality.

The reasons for the erosion of conventional morality are numerous and complexly interrelated: population movement from rural to urban areas, increased mobility (especially through the automobile), unprincipled advertising with its emphasis on pleasure and comfort, commercialized entertainment, changing educational and vocational patterns for men and women. But as a psychologist, I wish to single out certain other facets of the total situation.

For several centuries during its early history, Christianity appears to have been a highly redemptive ("therapeutic") enterprise for great masses of people. But, as a result of circumstances which need not be detailed here, the church gradually lost much of its healing power; and more and more persons who had embraced this religion found themselves burdened with guilt which their leaders no longer knew how to resolve.

People thus afflicted turned increasingly to physicians, who, however, were also unqualified to deal with them and who, for a long time, summarily dismissed them as "hysterics" and "malingerers." But the number and the suffering of these people increased until finally, in the middle of the last century, the distinguished French neurologist Jean Martin Charcot decided that they should be regarded as genuinely sick (he called them "neurotic"), and that doctors could legitimately treat them. In this act of "reclassification," as Thomas Szasz [1] has aptly called it, Charcot brought the medical specialty of psychiatry (literally "soul-care") into existence—and largely deflected the problem of mental health out of the moral and spiritual realm over into biology and chemistry.

But no one—including Charcot himself—knew what was to be done with these people by way of medical treatment. The new specialty therefore languished for several decades until, early in this century, Sigmund Freud advanced a theory which was consonant with the medical emphasis and which also gave birth to a specific method of treatment. The theory, as all the world now knows, was to the effect that a person becomes neurotic because his conscience is so strict that he cannot even *think* of certain natural impulses or "instincts," notably those of sex and aggression. This subduing of natural desires is called *repression,* which Freud regarded as the origin of mental illness. Given this theory, therapy called for some way to undo repression and thus release the instincts. This therapeutic method was what Freud called "psychoanalysis."

Because of the expense and duration of this form of treatment, very few persons could avail themselves of it. But the central thesis was in essence so simple and so appealing that the masses could and did draw their own inference: neurosis in adults arises from having been forced in childhood to conform to group mores. Therefore, if you do not want your children to be neurotic, go easy on discipline and character training. And if you suspect your own conscience of being a trifle too strict, it will be hygienic and perhaps interesting to pay rather less attention to it on occasion than you may have previously thought necessary. Hence, the pervasive cult of "permissiveness."

It would be tedious to try to trace in detail the manifold ways in which this philosophy has permeated our culture. It is evident in education, art, literature, law, theology, social work, psychiatry, and clinical psychology. But it was not until a couple of years ago that I came across its most blatantly logical application.

One day in Seattle, I was idly inspecting the paperbacks in the drugstore of the hotel where I was staying. The pictures and teasers on the covers of these books were so lurid that for several days thereafter, a kind of intellectual and emotional stench came back to me whenever I thought of them. At 40 cents a copy, even pornography in our affluent society is mass-produced and inexpensive!

---

[1] Psychiatrist and author.

In such material there is a deep depersonalization and dehumanization of the people involved. Characters have only a shadowy reality, and one has the impression of *mere bodies* moving mysteriously about. We are accustomed to and know what to expect from wild, even ferocious animals; but the human animal, bereft of his humanity in the service of either sex or aggression or both, has a quality that is infinitely more terrible. It is the horror we associate with "insanity."

It is apparent that in much writing, the cult of permissiveness has gone about as far as possible. The courts have acknowledged their inability to interpret and enforce obscenity laws. They cannot, the judges say, any longer tell where "art" ends and obscenity begins, and they also say they are not sure about the limits of "free speech." Besides, if sexual inhibition and repression are what make people "sick"—neurotically—maybe greater freedom in writing about sex will be therapeutic.

On college campuses today it is not at all uncommon for young men to importune their girl friends with the double-edged appeal: "You wouldn't want me to be 'sick,' would you?" What girl would wish to say yes to a question like that—and thus "reject" a little boy appealing to her "mother instinct"? A girl could say, "No, but . . ." And I am sure some girls still do. But the pressure on them is certainly in the other direction. And the theories of personality and psychopathology which young men and women alike hear expounded in our classrooms, see glorified in the movies, read about in novels and short stories, and sing about in popular songs, all point the same moral: If you don't wish to be neurotic, don't "inhibit" yourself.

Not long ago I heard a sermon entitled "Sex Is a Sacred Cow," in which the minister suggested that, as a people, we have become *sex worshipers.* This phrase had never occurred to me; but it was obviously and shockingly apt. Even money, of which we now have such an abundance, is not as important—at least we don't read, talk, and sing about it as we do about sex—and simple moral values are somewhere much, much farther down the list.

* * * * *

In psychiatry and clinical psychology there is today a growing emphasis upon "interpersonal" (moral) as opposed to purely "instinctual" factors as the determinants of personality order and disorder. Incidentally, this trend was interestingly reflected in a recent newspaper account of the selection of Miss America for 1966: "Miss Kansas, 19-year-old Deborah Bryant, a 36-23-36 sunflower blond 'bookworm' who thinks 'sex appeal is an unhealthy preoccupation of our generation,' Saturday night was crowned Miss America for 1966." This is a new note for a "bathing beauty" to sound, but it evidently sounded good to the judges—and to the American public. . . .

Whenever I lecture to groups of graduate or undergraduate college students on morality and mental health, someone is certain to make the following point: "But don't you see that we are really involved in a great *sexual revolution* and that past standards and tabus no longer have any meaning, necessity, or relevance?" A similar tendency on the part of clergymen was reflected a few weeks ago at a four day pastor's school in one of our southern states, when a distinguished theologian from one of the well-known eastern seminaries challenged me to show anything wrong with masturbation and homosexuality. This man was, I fear, speaking without knowledge of the sobering clinical facts.

The proponents of this general point of view do not say sexual *evolution.* That would imply development, unfolding, progression—and they haven't quite the audacity to make that claim. The word "revolution" means, literally, a turn-over, a change, with no implication of being either good or bad. More appropriate would be the term *devolution,* a turning or falling *down;* for there is little or nothing that is new in the so-called sexual revolution. It is, in point of fact, very old stuff. Freedom for unfettered expression of the instincts characterized primitive man's earliest experience, and that is what we've been trying to get away from ever since. The notion that this is something we ought to try to move toward is pure illusion. Morality is the means mankind has found for regulating the expression of sex and aggression so as to reduce interpersonal exploitation and conflict and permit peaceful, well-integrated group life and cultural development. Elimination of such regulation leads to retrogression, not progress.

When Margaret Mead, in 1928, published her book *Coming of Age in Samoa,* and depicted the happy, sexually uninhibited life of Samoan adolescents, many Americans interpreted this as the perfect proof of Freud's thesis that sexual prohibitions produce neurosis and that the way to eliminate neurosis is to get rid of the prohibitions and inhibitions. But what was overlooked in this regard was that the Samoans were, and are, a primitive people and there is a demonstrable correlation between their lack of capacity for self-discipline and sacrifice and their lowly cultural attainments.

Hawaii reflects the fate of another picturesque Polynesian people. Native Hawaiians, with their sensuous, indolent natures, have simply been no match for the Asiatics (notably, Chinese and Japanese) and the Europeans and Yankees, who have been trained for centuries in the virtues and advantages of industry, education, and gratification postponement. This is not to make an invidious judgment, but only to stress the point that there is nothing new about the "new sexual freedoms" which many of our young people are today championing. As civilized people discovered long ago, unregulated, unrestrained sexuality leads not to freedom but to bondage. It is the *control* of sexuality that is truly liberating in the long run, for it eliminates the confusion and obsessive preoccupations to which uncontrolled, undisciplined sexuality always leads. . . .

It is unlikely that one could find in modern literature, the arts, or even the tabloids anything by way of sexual "innovations" which the Bible does not mention. In modern city slums one sees instinctual freedom at its "best"; but the idyllic consequences which the liberators and reformers claim for it are nonexistent.

For some decades there has been abroad in the land the notion that all deviant sexual behavior on the part of our young people has come from simple ignorance and that if we would only give them factually adequate sex education, all would be well. A few months ago, at one of the mental hospitals where I am a consultant, I had occasion to interview an intelligent and well-intentioned woman who had nevertheless managed to end up as a patient. In the course of our conversation, she explained the lengths to which she had gone to tell her two daughters about sex, yet she could not understand why they were reticent with her about their own, obviously rather deviant sex lives. In the course of the interview, this woman made some painful but liberating disclosures about her own long-hidden, pathogenic sexual behavior. When I asked if she had told her daughters about *this,* she expressed astonishment that I would even suggest such a possibility. Characteristically, this woman had given her daughters a lot of "sex education" but she had disastrously neglected the education in *honesty* and personal loyalty which is probably the strongest deterrent to deviant sexual actions.

Because some other members of her family had also been hospitalized, this woman was concerned that insanity (conceived of as a disease) might run in families. I told her that there was very little evidence for this assumption but that secrecy often does. It is not what young people don't know in the realm of sex that hurts them but what they know and *won't tell.* Why should this woman's daughters speak honestly to her when she had not been candid and honest with them?

Today young people, particularly college students, are likely to talk a lot about "being honest" in the realm of sex. They often speak at length about the dishonesty and hypocrisy of their elders regarding sex, and say *they* are going to be much more forthright. Society, they feel, takes a very unnatural and "repressive" attitude toward sex, and they are going to have none of it. In a limited way, even the most conservative person will feel some sympathy with this point of view.

Adolescence is admittedly a difficult time, especially for young men. But our young people delude themselves if they jump to the conclusion that there is some easy and obvious solution to the problem. I've already alluded to the cultural implications of unrestrained adolescent sexual behavior in the South Sea Islands. And "child marriages," while having some very real advantages, have not worked out entirely satisfactorily in

China and India. Human groups the world over have searched and experimented broadly for the ideal way of regulating the mating pattern. All things considered, and given the kind of high-output society we all seem to want, our traditional pattern will probably be hard to improve on. This is not to say that we should quit thinking about the problem. But we must realize that the solution is not a simple one.

In their charge that our society is needlessly harsh, repressive, and inconsiderate in the matter of sex, our young people and some of their elders are really fighting a straw man. We have already pursued the cult of permissiveness far enough to see that this is not the answer, and even psychiatrists are beginning to stress the need for "structure" in the moral realm. . . . Laxity and confusion are the problems today, not rigidity and overstrictness.

So the notion that as a people we today are denying the reality of sex is absurd. More to the point is the possibility that we worship it. Thus the whole charge that sex is "officially hidden and ignored" is very wide of the mark. When I hear young people clamoring about the need to be "honest" and "open" about sex, I often ask them just how consistently they are, themselves, practicing this philosophy. They talk a lot about sex, but when it comes to candor concerning their actual *behavior,* I find that they often leave much to be desired. Although they level a vague and general charge of "dishonesty" against their elders, they are being dishonest themselves. When I have pointed out this incongruity to college students, some of them are startled and shocked by their lack of personal integrity on this score. Others say, "But you can't talk to my parents. They just wouldn't understand." What they mean is, "*I* couldn't talk to my parents about my behavior and *continue* it." As long as young people are still dependent upon their parents for support and the parents are keeping their part of the bargain, I don't see how they can in good conscience feel justified in taking matters into their own hands and making their own rules. When they do this, they are *cheating;* and this is a practice which, if carried very far, usually lands a person either in prison or a mental hospital.

Yes, a sexual revolution is indeed needed, but not along the lines commonly supposed. What we need, and need desperately, is a new and more discerning way of thinking about sex, and about the whole problem of personal integrity and morality.

What Do You Think?

1. Would you agree or disagree with this author's views? Why?
2. Which positions in the arguments you've read to this point seem most supportable? Least supportable? Explain.

ACTIVITIES FOR INVOLVEMENT

1. Prepare a time line showing important social events in American history. Identify the events which you consider revolutionary (for example, changes in clothing, transportation, communication) and explain why you consider them important. Judge the time lapse between events. How much time elapsed between events? Then hold a class discussion on whether certain times are more conducive to revolution than others. What characteristics do such times possess?

2. Investigate the writings on sexual morality, ethics, and behavior of earlier times. Select two periods of time and read a number of magazine and newspaper articles dealing with the sex patterns of each period. Now reread Chapter 2 once again. Should any of the information contained in that chapter be corrected or changed in any way? Explain.

3. Write a magazine article for an imaginary magazine presenting your views on the major question of this chapter, "The New Morality?" Let various members of the class present their views to the class. How do the class's conclusions compare with those in the readings in this chapter?

4. A Gallup Poll conducted for *Look* Magazine provided data on the following question: Many people say that there has been a great change in attitudes toward sex in the last fifteen or twenty years—say since the end of World War II. The following nationwide sampling was obtained: great change, 57 per cent; some change, 22 per cent; not much change, 13 per cent; don't know, 8 per cent.

Conduct a similar poll in your class and compare the results you obtain with those above.

5. Role play a grandparent, parent, and teen-ager giving their views and discussing the changes which have occurred in attitudes toward what is proper sexual behavior among young people today.

4

What Sexual Attitudes Exist Today?

People have different opinions about the changes in sex codes. What these opinions are depends upon the influence of tradition, rebellion, age, friends, parents, enemies, newspapers, movies, TV, teachers, religious leaders, gangs, and just living in society. In this next chapter you will be presented with the opinions of a number of different people concerning sex and its place in our society. Read carefully and then ask yourself: What are my views on the issues raised?

1. TEEN-AGERS AND SEX: A STUDENT REPORT *

In 1967, Seventeen *Magazine conducted a poll of teen-agers, the results of which were published in the following article. How would girls in your community respond?*

You've seen the statistics: one in six teen-age girls is pregnant when she marries; over 100,000 teens bear illegitimate babies each year; a shocking 200,000 have criminal abortions. You've heard the worried talk: young people are rejecting society's ethical standards; sexual experimentation is rampant in our high schools.

Now *Seventeen* has asked the teens themselves for their attitudes on the subject. In a confidential questionnaire sent to 2,000 girls, as well as individual interviews with scores more, *Seventeen* has tried to find out the truth about questions which trouble teens, their parents and society.

---

* Excerpted from the July 17, 1967, issue of *Seventeen* Magazine, with permission. Copyright © 1967 by Triangle Publications, Inc.

Three out of four girls—1,500 in all—answered the *Seventeen* questionnaire. They range in age from thirteen to twenty, and come from every region of the United States. More than three-quarters are high school students, 15 per cent have started college. A quarter of them are thirteen to fifteen years old, half sixteen or seventeen, a quarter eighteen to twenty. Not surprisingly, their views about sex, their knowledge and their activities change as they grow older, as increasing freedom and deeper relationships with boys pose more and more difficult questions, demand more and more difficult decisions. For many the line between right and wrong, sharply defined at fourteen, becomes blurred by seventeen.

A large majority of all the girls queried by *Seventeen* disapproved of sexual intercourse before marriage, but the percentage decreased among the older girls. A small, vocal minority spoke up for the new freedom—anything goes as long as you're in love. Others wondered, if intercourse is wrong, is heavy petting right? Will a boy respect you more if you do or you don't? Most girls wished they knew.

A significant minority said they were no longer virgins—more than 15 per cent of all the girls who answered the questionnaire. The figure approximately doubled in each succeeding age group: 6 per cent of the girls fifteen or younger had had sexual intercourse; 13 per cent of those sixteen or seventeen; and 25 per cent of the eighteen- and nineteen-year-olds. Almost two-thirds of the girls who have had sexual relations are still in high school; the rest are college students or out of school.

The potential consequences of premarital sex are not theory for teen-age girls today; they are cold fact. More than eight out of ten knew at least one unmarried girl who was pregnant. Yet despite much brave talk about the safety of the contraceptive pill, few girls actively engaged in sexual relations were protecting themselves against a similar tragedy.

Girls who answered the questionnaire were eager for more knowledge, not about how babies come (they knew that), but about birth control, sexual intercourse, sex drive. In theory, they rated their mothers the best source for this information, but in practical fact, many admitted frankly that they could no longer bring to their mothers the questions troubling them. These are talked about interminably with their girl friends, and the answers which emerge are often far from accurate.

Is premarital intercourse right or wrong? For others? For myself? This is *the* burning question, especially for girls over sixteen, for those who are going steady, are pinned or are engaged. One in four girls approved of premarital intercourse for engaged couples, but less than 9 per cent approved of it for couples who were merely willing. With each birthday, disapproval lessened: only one in twenty-five of the youngest girls believed sexual relations were acceptable for willing couples; in the oldest group the figure doubled.

The spirited defenders of the new morality summed up their ethical code: sex is beautiful when you are in love, but it carries responsibility —complete faithfulness, honesty and respect for your partner. Promiscuity is taboo. "As a casual thing, sex is wrong," a seventeen-year-old New Yorker said. "Kids who regard it as a fun-filled evening disgust me."

Love, according to these girls, justifies everything. A seventeen-year-old from Connecticut put it this way: "I felt only joy to have shared such a beautiful part of life with someone I really love. I have never done this with anyone else, because a girl shouldn't give herself to just anyone. We hope to get married when he graduates from college."

A Texas high school senior, no longer involved but unregretful said: "I have never felt guilty about my sex relations. It was something I wanted and did willingly with a person I felt very deeply for."

Yet many girls who were no longer virgins showed serious doubts about the course they had taken. Although two-thirds of them felt sexual relations were acceptable if a couple was engaged, seven out of ten disapproved of intercourse for couples in love but not committed to marriage, and a whopping majority—five out of six—believed it was wrong for couples who were merely willing. Some girls reported that they and their boy friends were struggling to end this troubling aspect of their relationship. "We felt so close, but we've tried many times not to do it again," said a seventeen-year-old from California. "He and I have decided (and prayed) that it won't happen again. I love him, and it's an expression of love, but we aren't sure, and we regret ever starting it."

Seldom were these affairs planned. Usually they just happened. "If you go with a boy a long time," a sixteen-year-old Florida girl said, "kissing leads to necking, necking to petting, and then maybe passions are aroused and it leads to sexual relations." Some girls, after such an episode, pulled back completely from the relationship. "It was the worst feeling I've ever had. I quickly stopped dating the boy," said a high school junior from Alabama.

Other answers from these girls showed their deep concern. Although almost half said they felt contented afterward, half were worried, and almost half also felt guilty or ashamed. "I felt sick to my stomach," one girl reported.

One practical reason for worry was a lack of precautions against pregnancy. Two-thirds of the girls who had had sexual relations had used no contraceptive themselves. With intercourse often occurring on the spur of the moment, most frequently in a car (the girl's home was the second most common place), opportunity for adequate precautions was often lacking.

Many girls believed that the essential feature of the new sex morality was personal decision. "Now that science has given us the pill," one said, "we no longer have to be frightened about pregnancy. We just have to decide what is right." This may sound fine in theory, but responses to the *Seventeen* questionnaire suggest that it just isn't so. A bare handful of girls having intercourse reported using the contraceptive pill to prevent pregnancy. . . .

Among the large majority answering the questionnaire who were still virgins, the attitude toward premarital sex varied a great deal. An acceptance of greater sexual permissiveness increased steadily with age. Although half of all the girls described their attitudes toward sex as similar to their parents', the number who said they were more liberal rose sharply among the oldest group. Few thought of themselves as more conservative than their parents. . . .

Many younger girls showed scant sympathy for a girl who became pregnant out of wedlock. Growing older, girls become more thoughtful about this tragic problem. Abortion was rejected by more than nine out of ten. "It's very dangerous. A girl in my town died from an abortion," a girl from a New York suburb explained. More than half thought that having the baby and giving it up for adoption was the best solution to pregnancy out of wedlock, with marriage of the couple rating second. A twenty-year-old from Illinois said, "Most marriages have worked because they wanted to get married in the first place. The one couple I know who were forced by her folks to get married were divorced just a year later."

Going away to college, or even visiting colleges during the high school years, brings girls into contact with new ideas which often shake the foundations of their established beliefs. A college freshman from a Chicago suburb reported that all her high school friends, like herself, had been virgins, but among her new college friends, one in three was having sexual relations with a boy friend.

An eighteen-year-old, formerly sure of her belief in premarital chastity, confessed that college contacts were weakening her resolution. "I visited a college for an interview last October," she said, "and a girl there mentioned a friend of hers who was sleeping with her boy friend. I just didn't realize these things were so readily accepted, but all the girls warned me, 'Wait till you get to college.' "

Asked their opinion on why some girls have intercourse before marriage, the teen-agers gave thoughtful answers, usually seeking to understand rather than to condemn. "There are as many reasons as there are girls," said a fifteen-year-old from Maine. Many understood such a step for girls who were in love, pitied the girls who sought sex out of loneliness, and were contemptuous only of those whom they judged promiscuous. A nineteen-year-old said of herself, "My reason? I'm in love," and of others, "Cheap girls can give no reason."

Love was the reason most often given for sexual relations before marriage. But half the girls who had not themselves had intercourse speculated that emotional causes—like lack of confidence, insecurity, a loveless home life—would be an important factor. And the girls who had already had intercourse knew their reasons for it; of these, a significant three out of five stressed inner insecurity, often resulting from lack of parental love. A seventeen-year-old high school junior said, "Most girls I know who have premarital affairs get little or no affection at home, and falsely think any boy who wants a sexual relationship feels love for them. I'd say a yearning for love is the answer."

Some suggested that girls who were unhappy at home used sex as a way to rebel against their parents, and a fourteen-year-old New Yorker explained that in some high schools, sexual experimentation was "in." "Kids think it's the cool thing. They want to go along with the crowd." To a Connecticut girl of seventeen, this was a very real factor. "Social pressure around here is unusually high," she said. "My town is very advanced. The result is that most girls think it's perfectly all right."

Do girls start intercourse merely out of curiosity? Some who answered the questionnaire thought so. A Michigan girl of nineteen who described her high school as very well-to-do commented, "Some very wealthy girls are bored and manage to get excited about sex." A fifteen-year-old from California added, "Some don't care. They want to have fun while they're young." Steady progression from necking to petting to heavy petting is also a factor.

Although the teens agreed that some girls have sexual relations to be popular, most felt that few promiscuous girls achieved their ambition. "You're certainly not going to get a boy friend that way. They would probably just scorn you," a high school junior said.

One important reason for premarital sex, according to the answers, is pressure from a boy friend, combined with a desire to hold him. "He says it will prove she loves him, and she's convinced by it," explained an eighteen-year-old from California. And a high school sophomore from New York said, "This happens with weak girls. If they want a boy to stick with them, they might give in." Yet few girls put sole blame on a boy for taking advantage of his date. "Sex relations are a give-and-take proposition," one eighteen-year-old said. "The girl has to have a part in it too. A boy will go just as far as a girl will let him."

Most of the girls answering the questionnaire were confident of their ability to keep a boy from going too far—if they wanted to. Younger girls advocated a free-swinging physical technique—slap him, kick him, knee him, learn judo or karate, threaten to scream, start to cry. But when a girl particularly liked a boy, verbal defenses were more frequently advised. "Just tell him. But it's harder said than done," commented a seventeen-year-old from California. A fourteen-year-old New Yorker said, "When you know a boy and talk to him, he knows what you're willing to do and what you're not. I can even joke about it. Having an honest relationship is the important thing."

Does a boy respect you more if you turn down his advances? Many girls who were not going steady were sure he did. "He's just testing you," one said. And from another, "If he really loved you, he wouldn't ask such a thing." But girls with steady boy friends realized that a boy in love could indeed ask such a thing, partly because of sexual arousal, and partly to reach a deeper mutual commitment. "Kids today are dating earlier and earlier," said a fifteen-year-old from Florida, "yet they're not supposed to marry until after college. That's a long time to keep putting a boy off . . ."

When do girls stop? How many neck? How widespread is petting? The questionnaire indicates that the answer depends largely on a girl's age. Ten per cent of the teens who answered the questionnaire had not yet started to date. But among the others, necking had started by fifteen, and petting usually followed within a year or so. Eight out of ten of all the girls questioned had necked, including two-thirds of the thirteen- to fifteen-year-olds. . . .

Fear of pregnancy was the only reason that kept one eighteen-year-old in the petting camp. "We do not have intercourse mainly because college is a long and difficult road without that added danger. We've gone together three years and have four more to go before we can marry."

Other girls who have petted heavily reported that they refrained from intercourse because of a shrewd assessment of their own immaturity. "There are times when I would like to go farther," said a fourteen-year-old, "but I know I won't. I feel it could be dangerous for me at my age. I don't feel I'm a stable enough person yet. It would be a bad experience, and I don't want sex ever to be a bad experience. You shouldn't ever do anything you're scared of. You have to feel completely secure with the boy and with yourself."

Girls queried by *Seventeen* range from this youngster, painfully seeking to cope with new emotions, to others, unaroused, still comfortably sure that temptation will never overwhelm them. "If a girl's brought up in the right way, she just knows what's right and wrong," a sixteen-year-old, just starting to date, said. "I guess your morals sink as far as having premarital sexual relations."

If a girl's brought up in the right way—is this the answer? Other teen-agers were not so sure. Girls who had grown up with consistent but fair discipline in homes in which they were loved still frequently found it necessary to question and to seek an ethic, not of their parents, their church or their school, but their own. *Seventeen*'s questionnaire asked the girls where they had learned about sex; what was the ideal source; and in what areas they wanted to learn more. Answers revealed that though there *seemed* to be many sources, they seldom satisfied a girl's need to understand herself in her relations with boys, and her need to establish the *right* way for her as a maturing individual. Girls learned more *facts* about sex as they grew older but found their curiosity about other aspects less satisfied. Often information was only half-digested, and misinformation was widespread. . . .

The basic aim of *Seventeen*'s study was to ascertain what teen-age girls think and know and do in this area which concerns them and society so deeply. What meaningful conclusions can be drawn from its results?

· Teens want and deserve much more information than is currently available to help guide them in a world in which sex mores are changing. "Forty or fifty years ago," says Dr. Lester A. Kirkendall of Oregon State University, "there was only one 'right' way. Now young people are faced frequently with situations which require them to decide for or against participation in some kind of sexual relationship." They need facts, knowledge about consequences, about alternatives, more understanding of themselves, their drives, and when and why and how these should be controlled. "Kids are taught that the egg unites with the sperm; this doesn't give them much guidance," comments a youth leader with the Ethical Culture Society.

Experts are convinced that more honest, open discussion is likely to decrease, not increase, sexual license. Dr. Kirkendall says, "The idea used to be to keep girls chaste by keeping them ignorant. Full and complete information is a better safeguard for a girl. Boys say that a girl who doesn't know the score is the easiest to persuade."

· Promiscuity is not rampant among today's teen-agers. Few young people have accepted "fun" as an excuse for license. Only a minority rejects traditional sex mores, and even this group insists on its own high standards of loyalty and love. Among these champions of the new morality, there is a dangerous attitude—a lack of feeling of responsibility for the potential consequences of their actions. No wonder most teen-agers have an acquaintance who is pregnant out of wedlock. For, through carelessness, ignorance or lack of availability of contraceptive devices, boys and girls who are having sexual intercourse are playing a tragic game of Russian roulette with potential human lives. Few seem to realize that for themselves, for their parents and for society, there is no happy solution to a premarital pregnancy. This is perhaps the most important lesson which teen-agers can learn from this article—that a girl who feels it is right to engage in premarital intercourse must respect the greatest right involved: the right of an unwanted baby not to be born.

· The deeply concerned answers from girls who have started intercourse or are seriously considering it indicate at least some awareness among teen-agers that greater maturity is needed for intimate love than many teens possess. Few girls who have had sexual relations said that it had made them ecstatically happy. On the contrary, many confessed to feeling guilt, confusion and fear. "Now that I've taken on these adult responsibilities, I suppose I must be an adult," said one seventeen-year-old. "But as far as age goes, I'm still very young, and there are times when I still wish I could put my head on my mother's shoulder again. It's horrible to know that you can no longer turn to her, because she believes one thing is right and you believe another."

· Many girls do not make a thoughtful decision about this important step. Casual sexual experimentation sweeps them into situations from which there is no easy retreat. Teen-agers must learn to consider each successive intimacy in the light of these questions: Where am I heading? Is this where I want to go? "If a girl wishes to retain her virginity," Dr. Kirkendall says, "she should know *why* and then make a plain statement of her wishes at an *appropriate time.*" Poised tentatively between the standards of an older generation and the development of an individual ethic, rejecting the first but still groping for the second, many girls do not really know "why," and even more lack the knowledge to recognize the "appropriate time" to start talking.

· How can a girl reach decisions which are meaningful for her in this significant area? Partly at least by an honest assessment of her motivations. For the purpose of sex is not rebellion against one's parents, nor is it to provide a haven from insecurity and loneliness. Partly too by an honest assessment of her own maturity. For as Dr. Mary S. Calderone, executive director of the Sex Information and Education Council of the United States, says: "Sex is not a relationship to be played at by children, but an intense and vital human excursion, admission to which must be earned by some degree of maturity."

What Do You Think?

1. Would you agree with any of the responses reported in this article? Explain.
2. Is there a difference in sex norms in college and high school? Explain.
3. From the evidence available in this article, what conclusions would you draw about the attitudes of teen-age girls? Explain.

2. WHAT DO TEEN-AGERS THINK ABOUT CHANGES IN MORALITY? *

A number of high school students were interviewed to find out their opinions on the sexual revolution. These students were interviewed individually and the answers each gave to the same questions are

* Interviews conducted in Buffalo, New York, and Denver, Colorado, 1968.

included below. In order to compare responses, the question is shown with each answer identified by the name of the teen-ager interviewed.
Sarah is 17½ years old and a senior in school.
Mike is 18 and a senior.
Bill is 15 and a sophomore.
Nancy is 15 and a sophomore.
Bob is 17 and a junior.
Susan is 16 and a junior.
John is 15 and a sophomore.
Betty is 17 and a junior.

1. *How would you define sexual morality or sex codes?*

Sarah: That's kind of a broad subject. Morality is just the way people feel about sex. It is personal—means something different to each person. Society has to make a lot of decisions, though. It is not just one person's actions, it is one person's actions affecting the whole group, thus the people should conform to what is going to benefit other people.

Mike: Oh boy—A system of standards established by an individual that work for him in society. It is basically individual.

Bill: It is like any other kind of code. It is set by the society itself, but is always changing from what used to be.

Nancy: How people feel they should react to each other sexually.

Bob: Being moral depends on hurting other people. I don't feel I am doing anything immoral unless I am hurting someone else or myself.

Susan: Established rules concerning your attitudes toward the opposite sex. Established mainly by teachers, parents, church.

John: Defined by society on what you should or shouldn't do.

Betty: Personal code as to certain actions you feel are proper.

2. *Is there a sexual revolution now?*

Sarah: That's what I heard, but it was just as dominant in our parent's time. There is more open talk about it now, and it is harder to set standards of right and wrong. The openness has made more stress on it.

Mike: I'm not sure. I don't know what was happening in my parent's time. In my personal life, I have had somewhat of a revolution within myself and among my friends. Superficially, it looks as though the public is becoming more open about it, but it is not important. If people's behaviors aren't changing, then it is not a revolution.

Bill: Yes. It is obvious in movies. There used to be censorship, but now it is changed. There are definite changes in the openness for discussion. As far as changes in sex behavior, I think there are some.

Nancy: It isn't specifically a sex revolution. Sex is part of it, but the young adults, 19–25, are revolting against everything. It includes young people against older people.

Bob: Attitudes at earlier times were about the same, but they were trying to hide it. The Puritan and Victorian ideas were there, but people weren't any different, except that now it is more open.

Susan: Yes. There is a lot more freedom in association between the sexes.

John: It is several different revolutions. In some groups there is more revolution. It is between youth and age. The younger generation has fewer standards and leaves more decisions up to the individual.

Betty: It has been so popularized that people think it's bigger than what it is. The kids talk a lot, but they don't do those things. Some people really believe the revolution, but there is more talk than change in behavior. A lot say they agree to more sexual freedom, but they don't really believe it. The ones who are different are getting more news coverage.

3. *What are the main causes for changes in teen-age morality?*

Sarah: I think it goes back to the war (World War II). There were different modes of living before and the war brought more freedom in all parts of life.

Mike: Scientific changes—the invention of the pill, contraceptives—sheds a new light on morals. An increased intellectual community in my age group looking at these questions and saying that the answers of twenty years ago don't apply now.

Bill: Part of it is another step in modernizing. The extraneous things are being taken away. Skirts are getting shorter. People are more serious and more alert to things and they want everything brought out in public.

Nancy: In old times sex was taboo and very personal. Everything is free now—Negroes are free, free speech, free love. It is a part of a change in society.

Bob: Parents are freer. They lived through depression and wanted to give their children a better life. Cars have also contributed to freedom about sex. Kids are taking advantage of the freedom. If my parents knew what I was doing they'd be shocked, but I don't think I'm doing anything wrong. Sex codes have remained the same, but application is different. When it is applied to others it is more strict than when it is applied to yourself. My parents probably didn't act any different than I and my girlfriend, but the public reaction may have been different. I have had opportunities for intercourse, but I never have because there are too many social problems involved.

Susan: A lot of changes in everything. Sex is just one area. It is a lot healthier now that sex is more openly discussed. Times are different now.

John: It is just a part of young people today deciding they should stress the individual more than society.

Betty: A lot of kids just like to go against something because their parents are for it.

4. *What effects do you think will result from these changes?*

Sarah: If some people don't smarten up, they'll be in a lot more trouble. A lot of them will hurt other people and themselves for later life.

Mike: I would hope that by questioning these standards something more situation-oriented in morals would result. There wouldn't be a Christian Ethic or Papal decision on this. It would be freer and more individual.

Bill: Movies will probably stay as they are. Behavior in schools will change and sex education will come earlier.

Nancy: It will be lost in everything else, because sex is personal. There won't be a high increase in illegitimacy. A change in sex codes won't have any real effects in the behavior of people, because sex is so personal.

Bob: No comment.

Susan: No comment.

John: There will be changes, but morality will go along with personal views.

Betty: It makes some kids think everyone is doing it, when that isn't true.

5. *Should there be some kind of sex standards for teen-agers?*

Sarah: Yes. We are worried about younger generations. When I was eleven, I was going steady, but my parents didn't know about it.

Mike: If you are raised with a questioning attitude, a parent can ask what's happening and not impose some social standards.

Bill: No comment.

Nancy: Parents should know their own child and if the child is mature, parents should be more permissive.

Bob: No comment.

Susan: They are too free now and the revolution has gone too far and it will swing back to more standards.

John: I couldn't say, because different people have different needs. Society has to draw a line somewhere, otherwise there would be anarchy, but I can't set rules for other people. Parents should see to it, by adequate discipline, that children can learn to respect parents and that parents have standards that children should live by.

Betty: Everyone should decide for himself what the code should be. The personal code should not interfere with other people. The code shouldn't be imposed on others, but everyone tries to. There shouldn't be censorship because a person should decide for himself whether to go to a movie or read a book. Teen-agers now are not immoral, they are just more obvious.

6. *What morality should govern premarital sex, illegitimate children, contraceptives, and abortion?*

Sarah: I think it is terrible that girl should be tied down to a child she doesn't want from a man she does or doesn't love. I could agree to contraceptives and abortion to prevent this. If sex is such a wonderful thing, it should be saved for marriage.

Mike: It is natural and healthy to have premarital sex. It depends on the situation. There are enough ways of contraception that illegitimate children shouldn't be a problem.

Bill: Premarital sex depends on the people involved. When the right people are involved it is allowable. If there is mutual consent, it is ok.

Nancy: Sex should be saved until after marriage because it is personal.

Bob: No comment.

Susan: Premarital sex is immoral, but it is being more accepted by my generation now.

John: Premarital sex in today's society is immoral. In adolescent society it is also looked on as wrong.

Betty: I don't think premarital sex is immoral. Illegitimate children are not good because of the way society looks on them. It is a tough life for them.

7. *How did you learn about sex?*

Sarah: I read a lot of magazines. I talk to my older sister and others. I can't really talk to my mother. It embarrasses me. I took a course in health in school last year. It was good, but it was three years too late.

Mike: The course in school was so late that it was ridiculous. It was also incomplete. Most of my education came from my religion which viewed sex as a natural and open thing.

Bill: A combination of sources. Sex education was started after I had passed that grade, but I'll have a health course next year.

Nancy: From my mother. There was no sex education in school.

Bob: When I was 13 my dad gave me a lecture—it wasn't exactly definitive. I got no information in school. We were supposed to, but the teacher said anybody could ask about sex and nobody did because they were too embarrassed.

Susan: Mostly from reading and friends.

John: A few years ago I went with my father to a movie and program on sex for boys and their fathers. It was mostly things that I already knew. I'm supposed to take a sex education class next year.

Betty: Mainly from friends. The health class comes too late. If you don't know what they are telling you by then, you're in bad shape.

8. *What standards will you expect of your own children?*

Sarah: After the way I snuck around behind my mother's back, I think I'll be more strict about morality than my parents were.

Mike: No comment.

Bill: I won't set any rigid requirements. I would want to have open discussions with my children.

Nancy: Sex should be after marriage and I would want my children to have this standard. If they don't, I hope they are mature enough to accept the consequences.

Bob: What I have had. Maybe more explanation of sex and that it is not wrong to have sex. I believe I'm going to have a tough time, because if I'm too permissive, they'll be too permissive and by then the codes may have changed again.

Susan: No premarital sex. There is nothing wrong with the sexual revolution because it will return to more proper standards. The revolution has brought out more frankness and a new, better morality should result.

John: I would tell them what I expect from them, but I would not say what they could and couldn't do.

Betty: I don't think I should have children. It's too risky. I wouldn't know how to raise them.

What Do You Think?

1. How would you answer the interview questions?
2. What consistencies and inconsistencies do you notice in the patterns of answers given by each person? How would you explain any of these inconsistencies?
3. With which answers would you agree? Disagree? Explain.
4. Why do you suppose some of the students refused to answer certain questions?

3. TOO MUCH SEX TOO SOON? *

The next opinion is expressed by Dr. Benjamin Spock, whose book on baby care is the most widely read in this country. He has also been active in social issues, including the Vietnam war dissent. What attitudes would you expect him to have?

I want to give my ideas about dating in adolescence. I should warn you, though you'll soon find this out anyway, that I was brought up in a strict, old-fashioned way myself. I still believe that the whole subject of sexual and romantic love should be considered primarily a spiritual matter and presented to children in this light. So this article will be useful only to [those] who take the same view; others may think it musty or even incomprehensible.

Before I take up dating, though, I need to give a sketchy review of emotional development in childhood. I'll use the word sexual when I want to put the emphasis on glands and crude, inborn instinct; the word romantic when I mean the tender, highly personal, idealistic aspects of love between the sexes, which is learned mainly during a childhood spent with parents whose love is of this kind.

Between three and six years a child grows spiritually by over-idealizing his two parents, and he becomes interested in romance, sex and babies. Between six and 12, through a complex interaction of emotions, he represses his interest in sexual romance, turns away from his parents and becomes absorbed in the impersonal outside world of schooling, social adaptation, laws and legends.

In adolescence the glandular pressures compel the child to be pre-occupied with sexual and romantic interests again. But the revived sexual drives will continue to be in conflict with the earlier repression for several more years, causing internal embarrassment and guilt and external awkwardness. The simplest example is the young adolescent's shyness in dealing with the opposite sex.

At first the adolescent doesn't know at all clearly where his feelings belong. He becomes generally intense and romantic in his attitudes toward different kinds of people. Yet he may be nowhere near the time when he can show these feelings toward an individual of the same age and opposite sex, especially if he is shy and idealistic. He may develop a great admiration for a teacher of the same sex or a hero of fiction. It's only gradually that the barriers between the sexes are broken down. Perhaps the adolescent first dares to think romantically of someone in Hollywood. Then boys and girls in the same school can dream about each other, but it may take some further time before the shy ones can show their interest face to face.

Even after an adolescent's instinctual drive has broken through the inhibitions of the earlier period and involved him in dating, a portion of this energy will still be held in reserve and invested in idealistic yearnings. Some part of this will ensure that his attitude toward the opposite sex is romantic and chivalrous. But another part, even at this relatively late stage of development, will still be sublimated into aspira-tions that on the surface seem unrelated to sex or even romance—to create things of beauty, for example, or to become a benefactor of mankind.

Before a child has become secure about his sexuality or integrated it into his personality, it remains a rather awkward, compelling, crude separate instinct. He feels a nagging curiosity about what sex is in the ultimate and a compulsion to find out by experimentation. These feelings run counter, of course, to his idealistic emotions. In fact, he may be tenderly in love with one person and still find himself impelled to make occasional advances—hesitant or bold—toward others in a rather impersonal, promiscuous spirit.

A child in the early teens is apt to experience a series of infatuations, in each of which the sense of being in love is intense. But he can fall out of love as quickly as he falls in. He discovers that he and his beloved really have little in common. Sometimes the reason is that one or both have changed. More often it's that they originally had fallen in love with the ideal they saw in each other, which had little to do with the reality. As the years pass they become more cautious, and more realistic about the kind of person they need and can get along with. As they gradually mature they also have more to give to each other—a vital ingredient of true love.

I myself believe it's better that younger adolescents (up to the age of 16 or 17, let's say) not have individual dates or go steady. In recent decades children have been dating and going steady at younger and younger ages. There probably have been a number of causes for this shift. Since the turn of the century sexual standards have been progressively relaxed—for all ages. There has been a widespread tendency to question the certainty of old religious and moral teachings and to substitute the findings of biology and psychology, as if Nature were perhaps the only reliable guide. Many parents, on the basis of their interpretation of child psychology, have been hesitant to use the same rules that were applied to themselves in childhood for fear of the reproach of being old-fashioned or of making their children unhappy. Some mothers have gone along with permissive standards because they wanted their daughters to be socially successful, above all. A few mothers have enjoyed vicariously coaching their young daughters in dating and then hearing the results from them.

I feel that early dating and going steady often cheapen love, make it seem mainly a biological rather than spiritual relationship. A majority of young adolescents don't have the maturity yet to love tenderly, generously, companionably, devotedly.

To a degree, they are willing to exploit a member of the opposite sex for their own curiosity and gratification, and to find out whether they can carry out—master—their own parts as beginning lovers. When young adolescents become involved in regular dating, the physical, experimental aspects of sex are apt to get a head start and crowd out the companionable and spiritual possibilities.

When going steady has become the local custom, young girls want regular boy friends—not really to love, in many cases, but to have regular partners at parties and to be among the successful girls. So they encourage or permit physical intimacy to hold the boys' interest. In becoming sexually aggressive in this sense, girls upset the natural, dignified balance between the sexes. And in becoming sexually permissive they often become involved in pregnancies that seriously hurt them and their boy friends—emotionally, socially, academically. (Illegitimate pregnancies have tripled in the last 20 years.)

By contrast, when a boy and girl are becoming more deeply in love because they are right for each other, the physical desire increases but is always integrated with and under the control of the tender and generous feelings.

The girl with high aspirations is particularly apt to want to reserve her full response and final intimacy for the boy she is sure she will love totally and permanently—even though this impulse is in conflict with her physical desire and curiosity. Many boys with high ideals have the same wish. When a true love is in the early stages of development it is usually the girl who, because of needing to be sure, keeps the progress of physical intimacy under control. And the boy is willing to let his ardor be controlled because of the tenderness and respect he feels for her.

Now, to be more specific, I believe that parents should specify, without being overbearing about it, the hour at which their children are to come home from parties and dates, where they can and can't go. Parents should know and approve of the others with whom their children are going out, and who is to drive. They don't need to be put off when children point out that they could just as easily get into trouble before midnight as after, which is a plausible argument. But the very fact that the parents set a certain hour, and are waiting for them then, reminds children that the parents are genuinely concerned with their conduct and reputation. Parents can rightly explain too that neighbors tend to judge propriety by the hour of home-coming, and that reputations have importance. When children have a party at home, the parents should be there.

Parents don't have to sound like suspicious detectives in asking about the plans and the cast of characters when their children are going out for the evening. In the 13-to-15-year-old period they should certainly know where their children are. After that they can continue to indicate indirectly that they still expect to know. If they have to ask directly and the child asks why they want to know, they can answer that good parents feel completely responsible for their children, at least up to the time when they go away to college or to work; society expects them to maintain that responsibility. "Suppose," parents can say, "there is some accident that delays you. We ought to know where to inquire or to search." Or the parents can say, "Suppose the parents of another child in the group call us because, according to their understanding, their child is overdue; we would appear irresponsible if we had to answer that we had no idea where you were or when you were coming home." Incidentally, if there is a delay or a change in plans, adolescents should call home to explain before they are overdue.

These suggestions of mine may imply . . . [that] parents can't trust their children and will have to admit this to them. Adolescents who are supervised carefully will surely reproach their parents for not trusting them. I agree that to admit to a child that you don't trust his morals, his character, is an unwise, tragic step. In a sense it gives him permission to be bad. He can say, "If that's all they think of me, there's no point in trying to be good. I might as well have the fun of being bad." Child guidance workers have learned how often an adolescent's delinquent behavior began in response to a parent's accusation or implication that he was seriously misbehaving when he really wasn't.

But it is not an expression of lack of trust in a child's character or morals when his parents keep some supervision over his parties and dates and hours. It's only a recognition that he is still relatively inexperienced about the many pitfalls of the adult world and still needs guidance, though he is at a stage in life when his pride and aspirations won't let him admit this. In order to make this distinction convincingly, parents must be ready for the reproach (about lack of trust) and answer briskly, because hesitancy encourages children to press their arguments and reproaches with more determination.

Some parents and professional people take an attitude about adolescent sexuality and dating that is quite different from mine. They say that we moderns have at last emancipated ourselves from old-fashioned puritanical attitudes toward sex, that adolescence is meant to be a time for sexual experimenting, that the availability of various efficient forms of contraception removes the last reasons for concern and disapproval. They advocate, for example, that all girls in their later teens be instructed in the use of the diaphragm or the pill so that there will be no misfortune of pregnancy.

This view is appealing, but I think it is too simple to be true or workable. The wish that some idealistic young people have, to reserve sexual intimacy for the person they will love deeply, is not just American puritanism. It has been characteristic of idealistic young people in Western countries for many centuries. There is evidence that the best aspects of civilization—the creation of all forms of beauty, the pursuit of science, the advances of technology—are fostered by the partial repression and sublimation of sexual interest in childhood and adolescence.

An example of the reason I stress this point is that psychiatrists in universities report that in today's atmosphere girls and boys who find themselves not ready, not wanting, to become sexually involved at this stage are made to feel abnormal by the taunts of their less idealistic friends. And if adolescents are routinely instructed in contraception, on the initiative of their parents or schools, it is an invitation to casualness in sexual relations. (Mature young people who have decided to have relations but have not been ready for marriage have managed, during the past half century, to secure contraceptives in one way or another.)

Some people assume that when a psychologist or physician speaks of inhibiting sexuality by giving young people idealistic principles, he implies some permanent lessening of their ability to have sexual pleasure. This is not what I mean at all. Young men and women who take an idealistic view of the real meaning of sex and prefer to limit their sexual experience to relationships that promise some lasting significance, or quite possibly to wait for an experience of true love, will have at least as much physical pleasure as their less selective contemporaries. But what is even more important, theirs will be the relationships that lead to lasting marriages.

What Do You Think?

1. When is an appropriate age to begin dating?
2. At what age should couples go steady?
3. Are the adolescents described by Dr. Spock similar to or different from those you know? In what ways?
4. Do you agree with Dr. Spock's views? Why or why not?

4. THE POPULATION EXPLOSION AND BIRTH CONTROL

The following data about increasing population in America introduces what is now a major issue in the Catholic Church: conflicting attitudes about the problem of population growth and birth control. Some people feel that the population explosion is the primary social problem of our time.

Population Estimates *

The prospective growth of population, and the uncertainty as to how much it will be, comes from the potential numbers of births.

* Excerpted from "Summary of Demographic Projection," Current Population Reports, Series P. 25 #38, March 14, 1968, U. S. Department of Commerce publication.

Population growth is the net result of births, deaths, and migration. Immigration was a major contributor to population growth until 1925. The immigration law of 1924 reduced immigration so that it is now of less, though not negligible, importance. The annual average net immigration was about 285,000 in the late 1950's and about 371,000 in the years 1960 to 1965 and is expected to increase to about 400,000.

Ever since the influenza epidemic of 1918, the death rate has been low. Until about mid-forties it was declining slowly, and since then it has remained relatively steady. There was some improvement until 1954, but very little since then. The rate is 9.5 per 1,000 population and is likely to drop somewhat, to 9.0 per 1,000 by 1990. To be sure, the number of deaths increases as population increases.

Births are the great unknown. They have fluctuated widely over the last fifty years and could well do so again. The rate was low during the depression years of the 1930's, was high just after World War II, and is now falling again. It was between 24 and 26 births per 1,000 of the population from 1946 until 1960.

Since Last Week: 1,250,000 More of Us! *

The latest edition of the United Nations Demographic Book provides some startling data for the religious conscience to reckon with in this season of dispute over population policy:

· During 1967 world population grew at the rate of 180,000 a day, or 65 million a year, to a total of 3,420,000,000 by midyear. If the present rate of 1.9 per cent annual growth continues, the total will double by the year 2006—just 38 years ahead.

· Three-quarters of mankind live in developing regions, more than half of the total in Asia.

· The population of mainland China is estimated at 720 million and is increasing by 1.4 per cent annually.

· Annual rates of population increase for other areas: Central America: 3.5 per cent; Latin America: 2.9 per cent; Africa: 2.5 per cent; Asia: 2 per cent; North America: 1.3 per cent; Soviet Union: 1.2 per cent; Europe: 0.8 per cent.

· More than half the population of North America lives in cities of at least 1,000,000 people.

· The world's four largest cities: Tokyo, 8,907,000; New York, 7,969,000; Shanghai, 6,900,000; Moscow, 6,422,000.

· Infant mortality has continued its downward trend, ranging from 12.6 deaths per 1,000 live births in Sweden to 150 or more per 1,000 in some developing countries. The figure for the U. S. is 22.

---

* Excerpted from *The Christian Century,* November 13, 1968.

· Life expectancy at birth is now greatest for female babies born in Ireland: 76 or more years; shortest, in Upper Volta: 31.1 years. Males in Gabon can hope to live an average of only 25 years.

· Female life expectancy exceeds that of men in all but six of 125 countries. In Sweden men can hope to live longer, an average of 71.6 years.

· In all parts of the world, married men and women have lower death rates than single, widowed, or divorced persons.

The spectacularly high birth rates in countries where the Roman Catholic faith predominates (and not in Asia, as is often supposed) may account for the disappointment of many Latin American Catholic leaders in Pope Paul's stand on birth control. For them it is more than a matter of private morality and clerical authority in relation thereto: it is a fundamental issue of social justice and revolutionary development. This tormenting issue clouds with uncertainty and potential frustration the most promising new joint Catholic-Protestant-Orthodox ventures in international development.

Catholic Church Moves Toward Biggest Crisis in 400 Years *

Turmoil over birth control is spreading through ranks of Roman Catholics worldwide. Stern punishment of dissident priests in Washington, D. C., is only the biggest of numerous incidents in what is becoming a crucial challenge to the Papacy.

All over the world—and nowhere more than in the United States—the Roman Catholic Church is moving into what is potentially its greatest crisis since the Reformation that took place back in the 1500's.

The new crisis centers on Pope Paul VI's encyclical issued July 29, [1968] which reaffirmed the Church historic opposition to artificial means of birth control, at a time when growing numbers of Catholics favor and use such means.

In London, an altercation developed on the steps of Westminster Cathedral between Catholic groups demonstrating for and against the papal encyclical.

In Essen, West Germany's Catholic Laymen's Congress voted 3,000 to 90 in favor of a resolution demanding revision of the Pope's pronouncement.

WASHINGTON'S TURMOIL

Biggest upheaval of all, so far, is under way in the archdiocese of Washington, D. C., with penalties imposed on dissident priests by Patrick Cardinal O'Boyle.

That turmoil began when 51 priests signed a statement saying that

---

* Excerpted from *U. S. News & World Report*, September 30, 1968. Copyright © U. S. News & World Report, Inc.

Catholic couples could, in "good conscience," disregard the encyclical. Later, 42 of the original signers and two other priests signed a similar declaration.

On Sept. 18, the Cardinal launched swift and stern measures to quell the priests' rebellion.

Penalties handed out to priests one by one ranged from complete suspension from public ministry, including the right to celebrate Mass publicly, to restriction of the right to hear confession.

Between these extremes, dissidents suffered a variety of limitations on their right to preach, teach or counsel.

It was also reported that the Cardinal had prepared a letter on the birth-control dispute, to be read to congregations in his archdiocese, which said: "Many Catholics, including some theologians and even a few of my brother bishops in other lands, seem—I say 'seem'—to have adopted what is called the 'new morality.' "

COMMUNICANTS AT ODDS

Laymen are involved in this dispute only to a minor extent.

A crowd of perhaps 800 or more persons staged an outdoor meeting in support of the dissident priests. A much smaller crowd of Catholics met to organize a group in support of Cardinal O'Boyle and the papal encyclical.

Mainly, the struggle among churchmen in the nation's capital—as elsewhere in the world—centers within the clergy. These include some who teach at Catholic University, an institution maintained by the hierarchy. One priest explained:

"Catholic couples can go on practicing birth control without making an issue of it. But a priest must preach and teach. He cannot avoid the issue if there is conflict between what the Pope directs him to teach and what his conscience tells him to do."

In that situation, a showdown appears to be developing between "liberal" priests and "conservative" prelates.

Some effort to ease the showdown was made last month by the National Conference of Catholic Bishops, which called on Catholics "to receive the Pope's encyclical with sincerity, to study it carefully, and to form their consciences in its light."

A later statement amplified this by emphasizing the duty of all Catholics to form a "correct" conscience and to recognize the "authentic teaching authority" of the Pope, even when his statements are not termed infallible.

The prelates' approach, so far, has not stemmed the tide of criticism from "liberal" priests and theologians.

In St. Paul, Minn., 76 priests wrote their archbishop that the encyclical might lead to infidelity and loss of respect for the Church.

In St. Louis, a panel of priests told the National Association for

Pastoral Renewal that many priests will leave their vocations if required to support the papal encyclical.

A Catholic University theologian, the Rev. Daniel C. Maguire, told the same audience that "the moral teaching against all contraception . . . was borrowed from non-Christian sources."

To deal with this clerical rebellion, which is being ascribed to a minority of young priests and theologians, some conservative prelates have developed a "hard line."

In Mobile, Ala., *The New Orleans Times-Picayune* reported, Archbishop Thomas J. Toolen called off a theological forum because some of the participants were among the 600 Catholic theologians in the U. S. who had signed a document opposing the birth-control encyclical.

Philadelphia's John Cardinal Krol forbade his priests to disagree from the pulpit or in the confessional with the Pope's view. Disobedience, he said, would be treated as "an insurrection against God."

In Los Angeles, a dissident priest was suspended by James Cardinal McIntyre. Six priests were removed from the faculty of the Buffalo, N. Y., seminary.

Growing numbers of Catholics everywhere are resorting to contraceptives. This has been especially true since the advent of the oral contraceptive—"the pill." Estimated numbers of users among Catholics run higher in the U. S. and Western Europe than elsewhere, but even impoverished families in Latin America are getting contraceptives.

Result, in the U. S., is that 52 per cent of Catholics were shown in a recent Gallup Poll to oppose the Pope's position. Sixty-five per cent believed it possible to practice artificial birth control, and still be a "good Catholic."

In the Netherlands, 63 per cent of Catholics disagreed with the encyclical. A poll in Britain found that only 43 per cent of Catholics there expect to follow the papal encyclical.

Pope Paul's pronouncement itself showed awareness of the dangers of a "showdown" that might result in mass defections. Vatican officials emphasized that the encyclical was not issued as an "infallible" document. One spokesman even suggested that future developments in birth control might bring a new encyclical some day.

Almost without exception, hierarchies in Western Europe have been treading a cautious path—a fact noted with dismay by Washington's Cardinal O'Boyle and with satisfaction by dissident priests.

In the Netherlands, for example, Bernard Cardinal Alfrink said that moral judgment would continue to rest with individual conscience —while stipulating that even noninfallible teaching of the Pope had an authoritative place in the formation of that conscience.

Britain's Catholics, on a lesser scale, are experiencing troubles similar to those of their American counterparts.

There, 11 "liberal" priests have been censured or suspended by conservative bishops over the birth-control issue. Now the hierarchy is trying to develop a common policy that will ease the conflict and encourage couples who practice birth control to continue taking the sacraments—rather than run the risk that they will eventually leave the Church.

A WINTER OF DISCONTENT?

What the Church finds itself entering is a crisis with deep dangers for the future.

Even defections on a small scale could inflict serious problems at a time when "dropouts" are increasing among priests and nuns, resulting in a shortage of pastors and teachers everywhere.

Unless differences over Pope Paul's encyclical can be healed, Church observers are predicting a long winter of discontent in Christianty's largest church.

What Do You Think?

1. What are the social, economic, and political implications of rapidly increasing population in the world?
2. What effects might population control have on sexual morality?
3. What moral issues are evident in the attitudes expressed over the Pope's encyclical on birth control?

5. A DIFFERENT RELIGIOUS VIEWPOINT *

This reading combines a religious view with the psychology of sex. What insights does it offer?

The physical changes which take place at the commencement of adolescence move the young person out into a world of explicit sexuality. The enlargement of the physique brings the need to overcome the awkwardness of the longer frame. It takes time to get used to a new body. Girls become taller than the boys their age and this tends to put them in social contact with an older age group.

Adolescents have mixed feelings about their new world and may adjust with difficulty to the role of adulthood. Turn of the century German psychology referred to this period as the age of *Sturm und Drang* (storm

---

* Excerpted from Donald F. Tweedie, *Of Sex and Saints,* Baker Book House Co., Grand Rapids, Mich., 1965. By permission of Baker Book House Co.

and stress). There is a sort of double bind on the young person. He is fascinated and pleased by the growth and development of his genitalia and his blooming secondary sex characteristics, but he is also troubled by how these will relate to the social world. The young girl may admire her budding breasts and yet tend to hunch her posture in an attempt to make them less obvious to others. Anxieties concerning the inadequate size of the genitals or breasts are frequently experienced by the growing person.

While these experiences are difficult enough to handle in general, the Christian adolescent is often under more pressure due to his growing concern for a godly life. At the time when he is becoming mature sexually, he is also beginning to mature in terms of Christian commitment and his vocational responsibilities. The tension of these two forces is often the despair of the struggling teenager.

THE DIFFICULTY OF LONGING TO LOVE

As the adolescent matures, he finds the new excitement and enthusiasm for life becoming more and more centered around heterosexual ("the other sex") interests. He likes to be around girls, to look at girls, is anxious to have dates and begins to think of being married. His fantasies of sexual experience are becoming more explicit.

Adolescents begin to talk, dress and act in ways that will be attracting to the opposite sex. Practically all clothing is selected in terms of sexual enhancement. Female fashions are designed with special care to highlight secondary sex characteristics. In different eras different parts of the body become sexually symbolic. Frocks which at one time were fashioned to reveal an ankle or an elbow were considered quite risqué and questionable for a Christian. Nowadays bikini type swimsuits are threatened by the advent of topless suits. The psychology of sex is such, however, that nudity, or the exposure of sexually symbolic parts of the body, is essentially exciting only when the body is clothed and mysterious. Fashions vary by gradually exposing hitherto covered areas and then covering up the "over exposed areas" which tend to lose sexual enhancement and mystery. The initial excitement of skimpy bathing suits, for instance, began to wane, and gave way to "Mother Hubbard" coverings which seemed then much more appealing. The current furore over topless bathing suits, a probably fading fad, is understandable in that it exposes the most important contemporary sex symbol. If this unlikely style should become widespread, the breasts might well become as commonplace as the elbow and just as sexless.

The difficulty for the Christian adolescent is that he is so sensitive to sexual stimulation and so desirous of being sexually attractive. He is also desirous of avoiding adultery, yet hounded by spontaneous fantasies of sexual experience. He is aware that one does not have to perform the physical act of sex to be in sin, for the Sermon on the Mount says that one only need to look (Matt. 5:28). The Christian adolescent's problem is how to have a healthy psychosexual development free from guilt and anxiety.

He (I use this in the generic sense, referring to both male and female) lives in a culture which explicitly appeals to his sexual sensitivity. Advertising is sexually oriented, films are leaving little to the imagination in terms of sexual parts of the body, or the sexual act, and the constant theme of literature is couched in the context of sexual appeal. An alarming increase in pornographic literature may be observed in newsstands. These media all tend to elicit sexual thoughts and desires in the adolescent. The great moral problem here, is not that these avenues of communication are sexually stimulating, but that they are stimulating to *illicit* sexuality.

Those of us who are rooted in an evangelical tradition ought to be very careful about our own relationship to a culture which we criticize negatively in terms of its exploitation of adolescent sexuality. Most of us have too little guarding of the TV sets in our homes (I am personally not so concerned about the trivia itself, but rather the over expenditure of time gazing at the "one eyed monster"), and are over careful for the sexually enhancing adornment of ourselves and children. We are in danger of being pots which call the kettle black. I have a friend, a Christian matron, who would not permit her daughter to dance for fear of the moral consequences, and yet bought her daughter a dress, the decolletage ("low neck line") of which was alarming. The good woman apparently believes that the male Sunday School students with her daughter (it was a "Sunday" dress), would be preoccupied with the lesson and not notice. Christian matrons in general, while often seriously concerned regarding the sexual excitement of their sons and daughters, or neighbors, purchase clothes that compensate for underdeveloped breasts or overdeveloped hips, paint lips to be appealing, fix their hair to be tantalizing, and scent their bodies with male-pleasing odors (and this preparation is usually in anticipation of being with social groups including other males, instead of the times when she is alone with her husband)! I find this not unappealing and am in nowise registering a complaint. I merely want to point out that Christians have no mandate to suppress sexuality, and usually, in practice, follow the cultural changes toward enhanced sexuality rather closely. They rarely are avant-garde, but they follow the vanguard closely.

There is no possible way in which to prevent sexual stimulation of the adolescent; it is a necessity of his sexuality. The hopeful task is to help him handle his stimulations and fantasies in such a way as to enable him to "grow in grace and the knowledge of the Lord." His budding sexuality cannot be repressed safely, nor ought it to be. Sexuality is a driving appointment. The need is that this be couched in a program of Christian sex education and orientation.

THE DIALECTIC OF LEARNING TO LOVE

The task of the adolescent, simply put, is how to look and not lust. This is not simple however. The energies of ripening sexuality are energies directed toward sexual fulfillment. This is as it ought to be. We are ordained of God to be sexual persons, and adolescents are in the process of selecting a mate. Sexuality is an important dimension of this selection. . . .

The adolescent should have many opportunities of fellowship with the opposite sex, but not so as to be tempted into sexual activity. Dating and courtship should provide increasing opportunities for experience with prospective mates so as to gain poise, social confidence, and some criteria for mate selection. This usually raises the question as to "how far to go" in physical contact and what kind of activities are appropriate for psychosexual socialization.

A wise, but not very popular, approach is to have little or no physical contact at all. Whether this is realistic or not in this modern world is a problem. As an external commandment it certainly breaks down. Young people in a church or school context where physical contact is forbidden have ingenious methods for maintaining the letter but not the spirit of the law in public, and ignoring the law in private. I have heard of one Christian institution where handholding is forbidden, and so the students hold toes under the library table!

I myself have no published list of "do's and don'ts" for youth. It is obvious that every aspect of bodily contact can lead to greater sexual stimulation and increase the tension for sexual fulfillment. At the same time, no form of ordinary physical contact of courtship necessarily leads to sexual intercourse. Physical contact with sexually symbolic parts of the body such as breasts, hips, legs, etc. are much more explicit in sexual advance than handholding or casual kissing. Kissing in embrace, however, places the whole body in sexual position and tends to overwhelm the young persons with sexual desire. Under such circumstances young men tend to become sexually exploitative. Often a girl is persuaded to engage in sexual experience as a demonstration of her love. Capitulation at this point very likely will end the relationship by the weight of guilt and anxiety. There is frequently a unique reaction to illicit sex experience parallel to the attitude of Amnon toward Tamar (II Sam. 13). The girl who believes that giving in will insure the relationship is likely to be disappointed, having lost her virginity and very likely her opportunity for marriage with this person.

The most helpful aid for the adolescent in developing his sexuality seems to me to be a positive approach. The young Christian person ought to be encouraged to see his sexuality as God given. His sexual tensions are also in direct relationship with the development of this gift. The expression of this physical aspect of love is to be full and free—within the marriage bond. The full delights of sexuality are to be experienced with the spouse of God's appointment. Sexual fulfillment has its greatest potential in God's plan.

This attitude tends to cultivate an idealism in youth concerning prospective mates that helps to curb sexual tensions, while at the same time helping them become more and better acquainted with the members of the opposite sex. Having an adequate knowledge of sexual physiology and being able to discuss this in the light of Biblical teaching aids in sexual continence rather than increasing tension. A young couple intending to do God's will, who are able to talk and to pray with each other about their feelings, and who exercise restraint in physical contact, will have a minimum of pressure for sexual exploration and exploitation.

I do not want to make this dialectic of learning to love seem easy, but rather to indicate that the best preparation for a life of conjugal love is to emphasize the wholesomeness and spirituality in sexuality to the adolescent. The negative approach of avoiding psychosexual socializing experience, because of inflamed desire, possible pregnancy, or the lust of the flesh has not been notably successful.

What Do You Think?

1. Has the author accurately described the feelings and behaviors of adolescents in regard to sexuality? Why or why not?
2. What is the relation of love to sexuality in American society?
3. How does a person decide among the pressures of religion, parents, friends, and his own conscience?
4. Compare the attitudes toward sex expressed by the author of this article with those of Dr. Spock in Reading 3. In what ways are they similar? Different? How would you explain these similarities and differences?

6. OPINIONS OF THE COLLEGE CO-ED *

What attitudes does the slightly older younger generation have? Pace Magazine *interviewed co-eds on a variety of college campuses to determine their feelings about sex and morality by asking questions*

* J. D. Scott and Jerilyn Hughes, "What Do You Want Out of Marriage?" *Pace Magazine,* February, 1967. Reprinted by permission of *Pace Magazine.*

like: "What do you want out of marriage?" Since, in the American culture, ideas about marriage reflect attitudes on sex, the next reading offers information on the views of older teen-agers.

Somewhere behind the silken veil of today's young bride are her hopes for what she wants her marriage to be, her fears of what she wants to avoid, her confusion as to how to be sure about it all and her clarity on maybe half a dozen steps in a journey of a lifetime.

What she reads doesn't help her much. Today's bride is faced with a tidal wave of cynicism about the contract she is signing; a titanic campaign, it appears, is underway to tell her she is licked before she starts, that statistically she hasn't got a chance. She is told that the only way out of the marriage mess she's getting into is to change laws so she can get an easier divorce, to work out a way to have temporary marriages to facilitate one husband after another like secondhand cars, or to live with a man as a common-law wife and have no agreement at all.

But in today's changing world where yesterday's immorality is called today's morality, one fact stands unbent before the gale—today's young woman, whatever her class or education or job, wants her marriage to work.

The easy-divorce peddlers use statistics of broken homes to attack the institution of marriage as being obsolete in a modern society. By the same logic it might be argued that because more people are dying prematurely from heart disease life is not worth living.

Hundreds of girls, mostly co-eds on campuses all over North America, talked to *Pace* this month about what they want for their married lives —what they are learning from their society, learning it often from the tragedy of their own broken homes or from the wreckage in the lives of their friends. They reject selfishness as a basis to make any relationship work, especially a marriage. To them the real issue of marriage today is what you put into it, what you want out of it, and how you become an adult in the process.

In spite of the reams of text in print on sexual compatibility as the basis for successful marriage, today's young woman does not give sex the first or even the second place of importance. Almost all, whether they have engaged in premarital sex or not, spoke against it because of its consequences in their lives. Most said it could only distort the way they want to look at the future.

"If you sleep with boys before marriage," one said, "what guarantee have you got of being faithful in marriage?"

"There is a lot more to married life than time in bed," was the general consensus.

The evidence is that a great many in this generation are fed up with the broken promises of sex and they are getting it back into its right perspective. While some still stumble heedlessly into marriage as a "warm nest of scented cushions," most young girls now look for the elements that will endure long after infatuation and novelty lose their luster.

Every woman knows there is more to life than body, more to marriage than a cozy home and family. Today's woman is realizing that the material benefits of modern life give her technical aid and comfort but do not give her meaning. She says she will be willing for her husband to take a step down in salary if it means taking a step up in satisfaction. She sees more clearly what is tinsel and what is gold and she is after gold.

The daily advertising bombardment of the "things" of life, the pages of editorial armtwisting and the temptation to conform to the group may obsess her mind, but cannot permanently satisfy her because they cannot crush the God-given mission in her spirit to fulfill the cycle of woman-wife-mother.

What she wants out of marriage is a framework for that cycle and the security that she can live it out. In the past the majority of marriages began on that basis.

But today's young woman as she looks ahead to married life in a different world is realizing that the woman-wife-mother role will never be wholly lived out unless she has something beyond family life to stretch to, something so high to aim at that the aches and pains of learning to live together become as insignificant as they really are. To discover and follow that aim is her guarantee of a marriage that will hold its luster.

That new aim and objective is the unique element that the young American woman is beginning to inject into the family life of today, modernizing marriage from sheer necessity and finding in it the best thing of all.

Coast to Coast—Co-eds Comment

HONESTY

"It's the only way to fly. If you can't be honest with the person you marry, whom can you be honest with? I don't see how you can hide anything anyway. He's bound to find out sooner or later. It is important so the relationship isn't seen through rose-colored glasses. Besides, I can't think of anything more exciting than honesty. You are afraid of the things you hide, and when you are rid of that fear you have the freedom of really knowing and caring for someone."

"I don't want to marry on any other basis. If you start off with anything hidden, then anything else that comes up you will hide too."

"If two people cannot be perfectly honest with each other they have no business being married."

"Honesty is vital. It is what saved my parents' marriage. To be honest to hurt or to clear your conscience—it's bound to be sorry and to stop what's wrong and start something new. With this, marriages like my parents' can be mended."

"I think a marriage built on deceit has very little chance for survival. Honesty is not a 'risk,' it is a necessity. I could never really love someone if I didn't trust him enough to tell him the truth." . . .

FAMILY LIFE

"The world is kidding itself if it denies that a good, strong family isn't the backbone of our country."

"People have thought for a long while that materialism would bring happiness, but we are finding out that it doesn't. I think the family should be so strong as a unit that there is always something to come back to. So many people don't think twice about their family. I think there has to be a certain closeness that is lacking today, to know that there is support when you are away from home. Families need to start thinking for each other, what they can do together as a unit for the community."

"TV, radio and the movie industry have pretty consistently presented a bad picture of the family. With rare exceptions, like *The Sound of Music,* families bicker constantly on film, leaving people the idea that strife is a normal part of marriage and even that they are abnormal if they *do* work well together."

"To me the most important thing in life is purpose. I want my husband to have it—a purpose bigger than money, security, self-advancement (that is, on a selfish level), or even 'family first.' I hope that I would work with him in this so that there would be no conflict between his goals and the goals of his family."

"I want to marry someone interested in the world."

"If my husband has the same basic aims and ideals that I have, mine will certainly be strengthened. I think this is one of the most important aspects of marriage. If you constantly have to be battling on the basic values you each live by, your own convictions as well as your marriage soon fizzle out."

"I won't get married until I am sure it is going to last. I want someone I can really work with—for something besides the marriage or ourselves. Then the marriage itself works."

LOVE

"Love goes far deeper than emotions. It has a lot to do with accepting a person as he is but then also caring more for what he becomes than for yourself."

"There is a difference between infatuation and love. You choose to love a person. It doesn't just happen; it is something you decide."

"I don't go along with marrying a person just because of love.

I've seen a lot of my friends do this and it just doesn't work. If marriage is really right for both you'll be able to work together for more than yourselves."

PREMARITAL SEX

"I used to think if it didn't bother anyone else it was okay. But I think now much more that there are certain high points in everybody's life and sex should be saved for marriage. To have premarital sex just pulls you down. When I have gone with a guy and it has been a purely sexual thing all I could think about was him. It kept me from doing the things I should have been doing and thinking the things I should have been thinking about. It uses all your energy in a very low way, and it makes much less of marriage. It creates too many problems."

"For so long we have been told not to have premarital sex because we would get 'in trouble.' Now that the pill has taken care of that, people are delving deeper into the real reason and to a standard more absolute than a law."

"There is always a nagging thought that if he will have sex relations with me he is just as liable to do it with someone else when we are married. It also produces guilt even though it seems to be more approved in society. The double standard for men and women is a problem. People do it but at the same time they disapprove of it."

"Because of false alternatives, it is pushed down our throats. We think we have to try it out. It leads to license."

"I think that the social acceptance of premarital sex is one of the major reasons that so many young marriages fall apart. A person who deadens his sense of responsibility before marriage cannot easily revive dead values later."

"Our generation has experimented so much and found so little."

"If Marriage Is a One-time Thing . . ."

DIVORCE

"I really believe that if people had to go through as much 'red tape' to get married as they have to get a divorce, there would be a lot more stable marriages. There would be a lot more serious thinking and planning, and fewer teenage and 'impulse' marriages."

"I'll make sure of my love and his *before* we marry. I would not consider divorce. It's a cowardly way to make up for a mistake you shouldn't have made in the first place."

"I think that you have to decide before marriage that you won't get a divorce. To make a marriage work takes *work*."

"Kids don't want to come from broken homes."

"Divorce goes against all I believe. I am from a divorced family.

There would not need to be a change in the divorce laws if we had more changes in people."

"A lot of my friends have gone into marriage with the idea that if it didn't work they could break it up. It's just legalized prostitution."

"Broken homes are caused by people who expect to get more from marriage than they are willing to give to it."

SEX IN MARRIAGE

"You spend only so much time in bed. There is much more to the marriage relationship. You can choose. So much of how you behave is how you consider yourself. You can be like an animal and require instant gratification of any want or you can choose to be different."

"I want to save sex for when my husband and I want to have a baby. Isn't that what it's for?"

"I think it is important in its right perspective in marriage. But I certainly don't think it unites people. If it does, then why do so many sex-centered marriages end up in divorce?"

MARRIAGE

"There will be differences of opinion everywhere from corn soup to cars, and I will have to learn to give and understand another important point of view. A marriage based on what is right, instead of who is right, has a 99 per cent chance of adjusting with flying colors."

"Marriage is how a woman can naturally and best use what she has inside her mind and heart. It is a natural part of being an adult, a step I want to take, but it is not an end. I think marriage is a new, larger dimension of living with new opportunities and responsibilities."

"For a long time I didn't want to get married because so many of my friends' homes were broken. I hated the way their parents fought. Their weddings were just a ceremony, and the vows later ignored. I could only see it for myself if it were a big success between the two of us with beautiful material things. But then I began to question what should come out of marriage. I think what I really want is to stick to the vows taken together and by this help to mend other homes. There is a lot you can get out of marriage, but a lot to put in."

"Modern marriage will include much more than just the two people. Because of the situation in the world today you can't just live in your own shell. The family needs to have an aim. You need freedom but based on certain standards and certain beliefs at the core—some solid basis from which to start."

"If a marriage is a one-time thing, a lot more thinking goes into it."

"I want it to be an adventure. I am not interested in marriage in a small set-up, just to look after each other. I want a partner who is someone who has taken on a big job, who needs my help to do it. What I am looking for is a pioneering attitude towards society. I look for an involvement in society and the world as well as our home."

"Marriage has got to be 100 per cent giving on both sides—in which case it is also 100 per cent receiving. Fifty-fifty won't work."

What Do You Think?

1. How would you respond to questions about the topics shown in the reading above?
2. Do the attitudes reported confirm or deny your ideas about sex and morality in colleges? Explain.
3. Do questions about a person's private affairs, like his or her own marriage ideas, produce different or consistent answers when compared with questions on the general state of morality or sex in society? What kind of support can you offer for your thoughts on this?

ACTIVITIES FOR INVOLVEMENT

1. Compare the responses of teen-agers in Reading 1 in this chapter with those in Reading 2. What differences do you notice? How would you explain such differences? Hold a class discussion on the topic of how true such attitude statements are.

2. Prepare a chart in which you place the attitudes described in this chapter in order, from least radical to most radical. Compare your chart with others in the class. What differences or similarities do you notice? How would you explain these similarities and differences?

3. Using the chart you developed in Activity 2, write short titles for each of the sets of attitudes—for example, the title "way out" for those attitudes you most disagree with, "with it" for those with which you agree. Write your own titles as categories for the attitudes. How do these compare with others in your class?

4. Develop an interview plan of questions you would ask to get at attitudes on the "new morality." You can use the questions in Reading 2 as a guide. Try the questions on some classmates to see if they produce responses which you believe are important and comparable.

5. Using the best interview plans in the class, decide on whose attitudes should be obtained.
   a. Conduct interviews with your parents, friends, teachers, and others. Compare results. How do the attitudes differ from those presented in this chapter?

b. Have different students take widely different views on sexual morality. Use the interview plan to see how consistently they can maintain their views.

c. Revise the chart and titles you prepared in Activities 2 and 3, adding the information from interviews.

6. How do you think church leaders in your community would discuss morality at a conference? Have class members interview a priest, a rabbi, an atheist, a fundamentalist, a Protestant minister, a Moslem, a Mormon Elder, a Quaker, or others you might select. Identify their basic religious and nonreligious attitudes on the sexual revolution. How do they differ? Now have various members in the class assume the roles of several of these individuals and then present a panel discussion on establishing a moral code.

5

How Are Culture and Sex Related?

Cultures differ in many ways—in their foods, rituals, traditions, and expected behaviors. Each culture has a set of customs and/or laws which have emerged as the culture has passed through history, and which determine socially accepted behaviors for its people. For example, eating with knife, fork, and spoon is socially approved in America, but is not the normal eating behavior in some cultures in Asia, where chopsticks are the prevalent eating instruments.

Differences among cultures also occur in the area of morality. What might be considered moral conduct in one culture is considered immoral in another. Even within cultures such differences are evident. In some groups in America, card playing and dancing are viewed as immoral, while other groups accept them as moral behavior. In the area of sexual behavior, cultures and subcultures (groups within a culture) differ on what is moral and what is immoral. What criteria exist for sexual morality in this and other cultures? Who sets the standards for sexual behavior, and how are these standards enforced? What behaviors does your subculture expect?

1. SEX IN DIFFERENT CULTURES *

Margaret Mead has gained fame as an anthropologist and writer. She has lived in a number of different cultures, studying their habits, customs, and living styles. In this selection she writes of Samoans and Americans. How do they compare?

---

* Excerpted from *Male and Female, a Study of the Sexes in a Changing World,* by Margaret Mead. Reprinted by permission of William Morrow and Company, Inc. Copyright 1949 by Margaret Mead.

. . . Cultures differ very much in the extent to which children are permitted to play out and experiment with their sexuality. . . . In Samoa, [it is] expected . . . [that] sex will be a delightful experience, expertly engaged in, and which still will not be sufficiently engrossing to threaten the social order. The Samoans condone light love-affairs, but repudiate acts of passionate choice, and have no real place for any one who would permanently continue, in spite of social experiences to the contrary, to prefer one woman or one man to a more socially acceptable mate. . . .

Marriages [were] arranged between families, with some attention to the wishes of the young, and the young in turn conducted with suitable partners the long liaisons that led to pregnancy and were regarded as appropriate preparations for marriage, and reserved quick affairs "under the palmtrees" for the unsuitable mates. Premarital affairs and extramarital affairs were conducted with enough lightness not to threaten the reliable sex relationships between married couples, sex relationships so reliable that they have now underwritten one of the highest population increases recorded in the modern world.

When we examine how this capacity for reliable sex responses that nevertheless do not threaten or disrupt a social order which is firmly built into quite stable marriages, we find that the relationship between child and parent is early diffused over many adults. The Samoan mother nurses her child generously, or if she lacks milk a chosen wet nurse nurses him; nursing is a slight but very specific physical relationship. However, he is given food, consoled, carried about, by all the women of the large households, and later carried about the village by child-nurses who cluster together with their charges on their hips. He is fed when he is hungry, carried when he is tired, allowed to sleep when he wills. If he does wrong—cries and disturbs the dignity of some consultation going on among the elders, defecates in the house, or has a temper tantrum—it is not he who is punished, but the child-nurse whose duty it is to keep him out of such difficulties and to lug him out of earshot when he cries. Children are too young to know how to behave, but they may be trusted to develop sense—*mafaufau*—in time. In the meantime adult society is protected against them, and they do not need to fear that they themselves, by their unsteady sphincter control, their loud wails or importunate demands, will endanger the normal order of existence. . . .

When children are five or six, they shift from being protected against the damage their own exorbitant demands and unregulated impulses might inflict on the dignity of life. The little girls in turn become child-nurses, who must themselves carry other babies out of earshot. The little boys begin to tag after the bigger boys, learning to fish, swim, handle a canoe, climb trees, and all the other lesser male skills. The girls' attention is focused on the role of facilitating domestic life and caring for babies, who are regarded as pretty tough and so more of a burden than a responsibility. The boys' attention is shifted to being at the bottom of a ladder of skill and virtuosity, eager to be accepted by the older boys. Permission to accompany older boys seems to provide a potent incentive to good behaviour, and the seeming miracle of transformation from demanding, uncontrolled, temper-tantrumish youngsters to sober little child-nurses and sober little water-carriers and bait-collectors goes on.

The break between the boys' group and the girls' group is fairly strong at this stage, and is reinforced by the strongest taboo of Samoan society, the brother-and-sister taboo. This includes not only one's own sister, but cousins, and of course all the girls of one's own household. Brothers and sisters must never talk together casually or lightly, must never walk together or touch each other, or participate in the same informal pleasure-seeking group. As a fourth or even a third of the girls in one's own village may be called "sister," this effectively divides the older children's groups bent on mischief and fun into one-sex groups. It also breaks the tie between child-nurse and young charge if the young charge is a boy. The term *tei,* younger sibling, is a term affectionately used by women. The brother-and-sister relationship is the focus of the male child's break from a lusty emotion-indulging early childhood in which he had his slightly older sister at his beck and call to a later childhood as a very small, very unimportant, very unskilled male in the older boys' group. The imposition of the taboo is left in the young boy's own hands: "when he feels shy, when he feels ashamed," then he will gradually avoid his older sister or cousin or young aunt who has so uncritically ministered to his childish needs. Nothing is enforced hurriedly; he simply learns, by watching others, by the remarks of others, by the looks and glances of those around him, that he is reaching the age where on his own initiative he sets a barrier between himself and his impulsive and irresponsible childhood, and declares the taboo to be in force. Throughout the whole period of childhood and early adolescence, boys and girls move in separate groups, maintaining their separateness by a certain degree of ceremonial hostility, sometimes verbal, sometimes in pitched battles with light missiles. Later, as each becomes ready, the girls are chosen for first love-affairs by older boys who have been initiated into full sex experience by older girls. In each sex partnership, one of the partners is expected to be sure and practiced. The only serious maladjustment I observed in Samoa came when two inexperienced adolescents had a first sex-affair with each other and became traumatized[1] by their own clumsiness.

The Samoan adult sex adjustment may be said to be one of the

---

[1] Shocked mental state resulting from emotional stress.

smoothest in the world. Passion and responsibility are so blended that children are loved and cared for and reared in large stable families that do not rely on some slender tenuous tie between two parents for their only security. The adult personality is stable enough to resist extraordinary pressures from the outside world and keep its serenity and sureness. The price they pay for their smooth, even, generously gratifying system is the failure to use special gifts, special intelligence, special intensity. There is no place in Samoa for the man or the woman capable of a great passion, of complicated aesthetic feeling, of deep religious devotion.

[*American*] *Pre-courtship Behaviour and Adult Sex Demands*

American parents are not primarily concerned with relationships to their children as members of one sex or the other, little creatures with bodies who are responding to the touch of their parents' hands or the light in their parents' eyes. Primarily they are concerned with their children as persons, as little potential bundles of high achievement, who must be given the very best chance, the best education, the best habit-training, for success in life. Life is a race that both boys and girls must run clear-eyed, sweet-breathed, well-bathed, with their multiplication tables in their heads, and feet that come down accurately on the mark. It is a race they must enter as soon as possible, telephoning at four, handling money, exercising and exhibiting competence in adult patterns. . . .

Growing-up does not mean to the American boy taking on the responsibilities and the trials of full sexual behavior. Growing-up means wearing long pants like his elder brother, driving a car, earning money, having a job, being his own boss, and taking a girl to the movies. A little petting, certainly, a lot of petting maybe with the kind of girl whom nobody would take out for anything else, but no one expects the imitations of adult behavior that are involved in dating to have results, either in a lifelong union or in pregnancy. Instead it is just part of the competitive game in which boys and girls demonstrate their popularity by being seen with popular members of the other sex. Success with the girls, if you wear the right hat or bathe with the right soap, is part of the personality of the young man who will sooner or later be called into the head office and told he has been appointed to that coveted junior-executive job. But just as the personnel manager will be glad to know that the young employee is a good date, he will frown upon the same-aged youth who has a reputation for active premarital sex relations. The love and success for which both boys and girls work and dream, groom their hair, clean their finger nails, study the etiquette books, save up their pocket-money and earnings, has extremely little to do with sex, or with the body.

The game is described as dating; boys take out girls, girls have to be asked, boys have to ask, both must dress correctly according to the adolescent styles of the moment, the date must be conducted in some way so that it can be known to the rest of the group—otherwise it doesn't count. The long association of courtship and costume through the ages rather obscures the issue here. Because dating and dressing are so closely associated, the assumption is that it is courtship. But men have worn war-paint to impress their enemies or their male comrades, and women have done battle against their own sex in pearls and ostrich-feathers, before now. The clothes, the flowers, the dancing, are all part of the game, but they are to be equated neither with courtship nor with behavior that is primarily sexual, although the pattern of dating does in the end have a profound effect on the later relationships of men and women in America.

That dating is primarily a competitive game in which publicly affirmed popularity is the prize can be illustrated by considering the behaviour of those who do not date, but withdraw, sometimes quite early in adolescence, to "going steady." For here we find two groups: young people whose stirring sexuality has been genuinely aroused so that they may be said to be "in love" with each other, and who find the game of dating meaningless because they prefer each other's company; and young people who, without being in love, depend on each other for protection, the unpopular girl and the unpopular boy, concealing their failure in the popularity game by pretending to prefer each other. Outside the dating group are much larger peripheral groups: girls and boys who are so physically immature . . . that they feel disqualified for this game where mimic physical readiness for sex is expected; girls and boys who lack the money and the clothes; girls and boys who have such a deep interest in something else that it protects them from wanting to spend their time in a game that is to them irrelevant. But for those who are allowed to play, the deep fear of deviance—natural offspring of our hurriedly assembled and slightly learned cultural patterns—keeps them in the game, demonstrating that they are successful in the way in which their adolescent social world, and every magazine they pick up, and their parents' expectation, decrees that they shall be.

But what effect on the actual sex behavior of Americans does the dating pattern have? In the first place, it defines the relationship between a male and a female as situational. You "have a date," you "go out with a date," you "groan because there isn't a decent date in town." A situation defined as containing a girl—or boy—of the right social background, the right degree of popularity, a little higher than your own is what one sighs for, or boasts about. Now superficially this may not look very different from . . . the "girl and a full moon" recurrent in romantic song. But the boy who longs for a date is not longing for a girl. He is longing to be in a situation, mainly public, where he will be seen by others to have a girl, and the right kind of girl, who dresses well and pays attention. He takes her out as he takes out his new car, but more impersonally, because the car is his for good but the girl is his only for the evening. This long practice in longing for and getting satisfaction from situations that are in themselves quite contentless will stand the American in good stead later, as he adapts to the demands of a new job, or learns to forget the companions on the old job because they are no longer part of the group to which he is expected to respond with continuous stylized warmth. . . .

The dating pattern affects adult sex relations in still another way. As a culture, we have given up chaperonage. We permit and even encourage situations in which young people can indulge in any sort of sex behavior that they elect. At the same time we have not relaxed one whit our disapproval of the girl who becomes pregnant, nor simplified the problems of the unmarried mother who must face what to do about her child. . . . We bring girls up to be free and easy and unafraid, without the protections given by shyness and fear to girls of many other societies. We bring our boys up to be just as free and easy, used to girls, demanding toward girls. We actually place our young people in a virtually intolerable situation, giving them the entire setting for behaviour for which we then punish them whenever it occurs. . . . Even before the girl has matured enough to respond to the cautions of her own body, she has been faced with the need for being the conscience for two, and at the same time playing gaily, deftly, a game that is never finished and at which she may always lose. . . . The younger the boy and girl when they learn to play this game of partially incomplete, highly controlled indulgence of impulse, the more perfectly they can learn it. There are fewer chances of the break-through of deep emotion, to confuse the learning process. But then comes marriage, with a different imperative. Now both man and woman must have a "happy sex life," defined not with the symmetry of dating days in which the girl and boy, in the same dangerous situation, joined hands to win together, but in which a happy sex life is defined differently for the man and for the woman. For the man, the demon to be avoided at all costs is lack of potency, defined in a number of quantitative ways—frequency, time, interval before re-arousal, accuracy in judging the strength of his own impulse. There is an implicit assumption for males that if one copulates one is happy. The sort of sex life that was once placed outside marriage, in the redlight district of the nineties, has to a degree been imported into it. Now, as then, the man is not schooled in any elaborations; technique, even if learned, is to a degree learned unwillingly and despised. But during the period when the split was closing between the good woman—whom one married and respected, and did not expect to take liberties with—and the bad woman—to whom one repaired for physical relief and whose allure was regarded merely as an aid to rapid sexual desire—the new patterns of dating and petting were developing. A tremendous clamour arose in the literature in England and America about women's need for and right to the same sort of sexual satisfaction that men have.

This clamour was heavily disguised as an exploration of the female psyche, which revealed that women were as much in need of sexual pleasure as men. The white-bearded, saintly-faced men who wrote and worked to get acceptance for this point of view certainly felt like Santa Clauses dispensing blessings and largess where there had been dearth and deprivation before. The news spread, and about the time of World War I this emphasis coincided with the loosening of sex controls and the entrance of women in greater and greater numbers into industry. Good women became women who should enjoy sex, and enjoy it in a way that is definitely analogous to male enjoyment. Now this is not an untenable way of viewing sex behaviour. Both in France and in Samoa, happy sex relationships are postulated on the male's taking pride and pleasure in gratifying the female, in inducing in her a climax behaviour comparable to his own. In neither Samoa nor France is simple copulation expected to produce such results. We might possibly have shifted from the Puritan position in which good women took no pleasure in sex, and bad women took no pleasure in anything else, to a philosophy and a practice in sex in which men learned a variety of ways of evoking climactic behaviour in women. But a second influence—almost as strong as the first—entered the scene. This was the doctrine that women should have climaxes just like men, and they should get them not by learned responsiveness, but from the simple act of copulation. If they did not, they were voted as frigid by a psychiatry in which a European male version of sex differences was very influential. Yet there seems no reason to believe that climactic responses to simple copulation are "natural" to all women, or even to any large proportion of women.

So we now have a very complicated set of standards of sex adjustment that have been developing side by side with the change in adolescent sex behavior, but are not very well integrated with it. During adolescence, the male learns to let his direct potency be checked by a girl who learns not to be moved beyond the point of control. Then in marriage they are faced with the demand that he be simply and directly potent, and that she experience climactic satisfaction from his simple, unelaborated potency. Returns to the procedures of petting are suspect as regression on both their parts. The husband resents interference with the display of his potency, now an index of his successful masculinity. The wife feels inadequate if she insists on substitute gratifications, and if she is not swept away—after years of learning not to be swept away. Yet the complete total relaxation of feminine surrender, as distinguished from specific orgasmic behaviour, is hardly available to women who have had to live through years of bridling their every impulse to yield and surrender.

These discrepancies between the demands that are made on very young boys and girls to act out and yet control a whole series of hetero-sexual activities, and the later standards that cause so many marriages to fail to supply what amounts to an impossible demand for sexual happiness, are not surprising. Success in marital sexual happiness now becomes a duty like every other success-demand in America. American culture has grown up so fast, and been compounded from so many sources, that the presence of contradictions such as are found even in much older and more integrated cultures is to be expected. But it does seem important to realize that the more successfully young adolescents deal with the difficult problems of freedom and demanded dating, the less prepared they are to meet the particular criteria for sex adjustment in marriage.

What Do You Think?

1. What are the characteristics of Samoan sexuality which are different from American? The book from which this excerpt was taken was written in 1949. Are there any comments on American sexual patterns that are no longer valid? Explain.
2. What rituals in sexual behavior of American adolescents are similar in meaning to those of Samoan youth?
3. Are the criteria for sexual morality in each culture suitable ones? Explain your reasoning.
4. Would you agree with the thought expressed in the last sentence in this reading? Why or why not?

2. MORALITY AND THE ENGLISH TEEN-AGER *

The next reading suggests further the confusion and hypocrisy that many adults display when they communicate what they expect of or feel about teen-age sexual activity. What causes the type of adult behavior shown here?

Teacher: . . . and so you will realize that sex is not something to be taken lightly. It's something to be kept for marriage. Your mothers

---

* Excerpted from John Wilson, *Logic and Sexual Morality,* Penguin Books, Ltd., London, England.

and fathers are decent people: they expect you to be in at a reasonable hour in the evening, not to be out all night kissing and petting. Of course there's nothing wrong with sex, it can be a source of great pleasure: but you've got to be responsible about it, take a mature and grown-up attitude towards it. No girl wants to take the risk of getting into trouble, and no right-minded boy would want her to take it. Now, if any of you have any problems, there's Canon Phillips down at the church or Miss Snaith on the Moral Welfare Committee, they'll be only too pleased to help . . .

Meanwhile, something like this was going on in the minds of the audience:

Girl: . . . The same old stuff you read in the magazines on the problem page . . . I wonder what Robin Williams thinks of it all, I do like him, will he take me to the Palais tonight . . . coo, my ma and pa are adult and responsible all right, they don't seem to have any sex at all any more . . . great pleasure, well yes it's exciting with Robin, only he keeps trying to do funny things with me, I don't want to offend him though, otherwise he'll take Sylvia instead . . . no, I don't want to get into trouble, do you think those life pills really work, anyway we needn't go all the way . . . oh lord, not Miss Snaith, what does she know about it, I bet no one's ever made love to her, I mean not ever . . .

Boy: . . . I've heard all this before, what's all the fuss about . . . kept for marriage, that's silly, I don't want to marry someone who doesn't like making love like Jennifer, do I . . . what's a grown-up attitude anyway, grown-ups don't seem to do so well at it . . . what does *he* know about great pleasure, I bet he's never had a girl like Sylvia, coo the things she says when I get her in the car . . . hasn't ever heard of contraceptives, the silly idiot . . . am I a right-minded boy, I don't know, all my friends seem to do the same, I mean it's only natural isn't it . . .

It should also be said that about 5 per cent of the audience were reading books under their desks (Ian Fleming, Mickey Spillane, "Valentine," and "Hollywood Stories"); about 16 per cent were thinking about sex, but along quite different and more direct lines; and about 20 per cent were not listening at all.

This sort of talk and audience-reaction are not unusual, and if the latter is considered unsatisfactory, it should certainly not be put down to the fault of the teacher. All things considered—and I do not intend to sound patronizing, because I have tried it and know the difficulties involved—he was doing his job very well. It points rather to the conspiracy of silence and the lack of communication which I am trying to characterize.

In February of 1962 I attended a sort of Brains Trust at a grammar school, to which the audience of teenagers and their parents put questions about sex, religion, and morality. The kind of questions that came from the parents were:

"Would the panel say why so few children today seem to absorb what we teach them about religion and morality?", "Since we are all agreed that the Christian attitude to sex can be the only right one, why is there so much dispute about what to teach our children?", "What does the panel suggest can be done to stop the flood of provocative and pornographic literature and films which seduce the present generation?", and so on. The headmaster, also a member of the Brains Trust, was frankly amazed at these questions. He knew the parents well. Very few of them were practising Christians, and practically none of them were absolutely clear in their own minds about the reasons for and against various types of sexual behaviour. Yet in the twinkling of an eye, and with a unanimity at once admirable and pathetic, they pretended to a solid front of orthodox morality, in the passionate desire entertained by almost all parents that their children should be more respectable than themselves. Their own behaviour-patterns and principles (in so far as they had any clear principles at all) were so totally unlike their questions that it was difficult to believe them to be the same parents that consulted him, in private, about the most intimate matters relating to their own lives and those of their sons. A woman whose question read "How are we to teach young people today that the family must come first?" had appeared in the headmaster's study three days before, proclaiming that she was about to desert her husband for a lover with whom she had been sleeping for the last two years.

Under these circumstances it was not surprising that the teenagers present did not ask many questions. The only ones forthcoming were devised by a capable prefect who felt that the show must go on, and took comparatively harmless forms such as "Does the panel think that the increased divorce rate is due to the last war?" or "In what ways do the children of broken homes suffer?" Afterwards I collected the slips of paper on which the teenagers had written their questions, which another prefect rather reluctantly relinquished. They contained questions like "Is it in fact true that men prefer their wives to be virgins on marriage? I don't and none of my friends do. Are we in the minority?", "Can you really know whether you want to marry a girl before you sleep with her?", and "Aren't there some societies which are just as good as ours but practise quite different sexual moralities?" These seemed to me intelligent questions; but of course they never had a chance, and the teenagers were quite right to withdraw them.

In case it should be thought that I am merely making fun of a form of communication which should essentially be private by picking on public examples, let me now quote from a recording made of a private conversation between a girl of sixteen and her parents:

Mother: Why don't you ever talk to us about things, Betty? You must have some problems, you came in ever so unhappy last night. Tell your mum what it is dear. (*Silence.*)

Father: If it's about George, I can speak to him if you like, you know: it's often helpful—

Girl: Please, Dad, don't. (*Silence.*)

Father: Well, what is it then?

Girl: I don't *want* to talk about it, why should I?

Mother: Well, naturally we're worried about you, Betty, you don't seem yourself these days. Is it something you don't know about your own body, dear, or—

Girl: Oh, mum, I learned all that years ago. No, it's just that—oh, I don't know, I feel all sorts of things when George—oh, I don't know. (*Silence.*)

Mother: You should be having fun, dear, before you settle down and get married, you know we're looking forward to your finding some nice man—

Girl: Yes, I know what *you* want, you want me to grow up the same as you, and live in a dull old house and get all the meals and not have any sex or passion or anything—oh, it's no good talking to you, you've got your lives, you aren't going to change—

Mother: We haven't done too badly, dear, not really.

Girl: I know, mum, but it's all so difficult, there's so much I want, the books are no good, nobody tells the truth . . .

Father: Well, when I was your age, Betty, I made your mother much happier than this boy seems to make you.

Girl: Did you? Did he, mum?

Mother: Well, I don't know, dear, of course there were some difficulties, I can't really remember.

Girl: Oh, it's no good talking to you.

Finally, a conversation I had about a year ago with a boy in my house at The King's School, Canterbury. He was a very able boy, who had already got an award to an Oxford college, and had come in originally to ask how he should spend his time at Oxford:

Boy: And what about girls, sir?

Me: Well, *what* about them?

Boy: I mean, how much time should one spend on them?

Me: Well, you're not homosexually inclined, so far as I know, so I should think you'd probably want to spend some time on them, wouldn't you?

Boy: Yes, but what I mean is, should one sleep with them or not?

Me: It depends on all sorts of things. What do you think?

Boy: I know what *I* think, I want to know what *you* think.

Me (evasively): Well, I think one should be very careful about all this, I mean, one doesn't want to hurt people's feelings, and it isn't just a game, you know, and—

Boy: Yes, well, you're paid to say that sort of thing, aren't you? I mean, the parents wouldn't like it if you told us that sleeping with girls was quite O.K., provided you were careful about everything.

Me: O.K., then why ask?

Boy: Oh, I thought you might be inclined to tell the truth for a change. I mean, you know as well as I do that all the points against don't really add up to a complete prohibition. First, contraceptives and other methods can make it quite safe. Second, girls don't by any means always suffer—often they are helped by it psychologically. Third, so far from spoiling one's future marriage it assists one to make a wise choice. Fourth, lots of other societies do it and it doesn't seem to do them any harm; on the contrary, consider Polynesia before the missionaries came along—a much better sexual atmosphere than ours, Fifth—

Me: O.K., so you know all this, so O.K. Why come to me?

Boy: Well, as I say, I thought you might give me one or two tips about how to handle girls. You know, how to seduce them without hurting them, and so forth.

Me: No, I don't really think I can—

Boy: Oh, well, thanks for the coffee, anyway.

I do not wish to multiply examples indefinitely, and only quote the above in an attempt to add a touch of realism to a subject which very easily degenerates into a series of moral platitudes, statistics, and pious expression of belief. At the time I collected these illustrations, educational authorities from *The Times Educational Supplement* downwards were feeling vaguely that they ought to do something about the sex problem in schools. Encouraged by the exhortations of such members of the Christian faith who had nothing better to do, and spurred into action by tales of schoolgirls with contraceptives in their handbags, they decided, in certain areas at least, to launch a campaign, not so much in a fervour of moral righteousness, as with a rather ill-defined feeling that the public would expect something to be done. ("Of course it's not as bad as people make out, but I suppose we ought to do *something*," as one Director of Education said.) What they did was to send round various members of the church or the medical profession to the schools in their area to Talk to the Children About Sex. These talks usually lasted about an hour, and were attended by the whole school. I heard quite a few of these talks. One or two were quite sensible, but of course cut no real ice. Most were completely off any point which could conceivably have worried the children. Some were grotesque, and would have been funny had they not been tragic. I cannot resist quoting a few of the remarks:

"We all know, of course, that homosexuality stunts the growth of the human spirit" (this to an audience including sixth-form classicists who had just read Plato's *Symposium*).

"Remember that children from broken homes will always suffer from weak personalities" (three senior prefects, perhaps the most competent and happiest boys their school has ever had, being present—all from broken homes).

"Some of you will be worrying about what happens when you approach the age of puberty" (this to a group of 16-year-olds).

"What the New Testament says about sex is only common sense, and any decent person knows in his heart that it is true" (the audience on this occasion was international, and included three Chinese boys, a Hindu girl, and two Somalis).

"No really great author needs to use obscene language" (unfortunately some of the boys had done Shakespeare's *Troilus and Cressida* as a set text).

"When women reach the age of about forty-five, sex becomes unimportant" (at this point my mother walked out). . . .

While this vague but rather frightening recrudescence [1] of second-hand Puritanism was going on in the schools, the correspondence columns of *The Times*—a journal unfortunately not widely read by teenagers—contained all sorts of letters about statistics for sex crimes, the divorce rate, earlier puberty, broken homes, and so on. Meanwhile the flood of books from the presses, fulminating, advising, analysing, denouncing, reassuring, and being terribly sensible about the sex problem, became even more copious than usual, and could be seen in large numbers on the bookstalls among the other paperbacks—*Forever Amber* side by side with *Common-sense about Sex,* and *The Difficulties of Adolescence* jostling *Lady Chatterley*. At the same time the romantic magazines for girls, particularly those consisting almost entirely of strip cartoons such as *Marilyn* and *Valentine,* and the more direct and quasi-pornographic literature for the male sex, maintained their usual immense circulation. At the same time, too, in cars, woods, fields, back rooms, flatlets, and

[1] Breaking out afresh.

beaches, adolescents and adults continued to kiss, pet, and sometimes even sleep with each other; parents and schoolmasters continued to worry and deprecate; the churches continued to lament the decay of religion and morality; and the technology on which our society is based continued, inevitably, to make money the measure of all things.

All this presents a fairly horrifying picture; more horrifying, however, in its demonstration of our total inability to talk, think, or feel straight about sex than in any moral aspect which this or that person, with this or that particular axe to grind, might care to assign to it. We are like children trying to teach each other how to play a game, without knowing what the game is, what its rules are, how to explain them to the other children, or even whether the other children want to play. Nor is our own age or our own society unique in these respects. The confusion which baffles and frightens us, filling us with despair, pity, or anger, according to our natures, has occurred before, and is occurring now in other societies still staggering beneath the hammer-blows of a new technology or new social conditions for which their individual upbringing and mental outlook is proving quite inadequate.

What Do You Think?

1. From this reading, what can you infer about sex education in England?
2. Do you agree with the author's portrayal of a "horrifying picture" in teaching sexual morality? Why or why not?
3. Might examples similar to the ones presented by the author be found in America? If so, how would you explain this?
4. Would you agree or not with the author that "almost all parents [desire] that their children should be more respectable than themselves"? Explain.

ACTIVITIES FOR INVOLVEMENT

1. Develop a list of dating behaviors you consider moral in American society. Rate each of the behaviors according to the following scale:
   1. Unquestionably moral in America.
   2. Accepted as moral by traditional approval.
   3. Accepted as moral by older generations.
   4. Accepted as moral by younger generation.
   5. Accepted as moral by avant-garde.
   6. Questionable morality in America.

   Compare your ratings with those of your classmates. How did various people decide? What criteria were used?

2. Assume that you are a member of the ruling body in a hypothetical society. It is your duty to establish a set of moral codes to govern the sexual behavior of members of that society. Draw up a list of things you believe that you will need to know about other aspects of the customs of the hypothetical society in order to develop rules of sexual morality. Compare your list with those made by your classmates. Then discuss, What are the most influential customs outside of sex that assist in establishing proper sexual conduct in a society? The least influential?

3. Use your imagination to create a culture with some established customs and taboos as determined in Activity 2. Prepare a set of socially approved sex codes which are consistent with the established customs. Explain why you chose the sex codes that you did in class discussion and then alter those parts of the code which are shown to be inconsistent. What codes are intended to apply to all members of the society regardless of age, beliefs, sex, or mental and physical condition? Why? What codes are intended to apply to only some members of the society? Why? Write a short paper explaining how your code can be changed. Enforced?

4. In comparing the hypothetical societies and sex codes in your class, invent a culture which has the support of the majority of class members. What are the basic accepted behavior patterns? What do you plan to do for those members of the class who do not agree with the majority? Would your moral codes be acceptable in America or Samoa or any other society that you know about? Why or why not?

5. Assume that the following persons have arrived in your hypothetical culture to live and study the sex behaviors of youngsters. Write a page or two in an imaginary journal in which you report on the observations of one or more of these individuals.
   a. A strongly religious Puritan missionary.
   b. A member of a Peace Corps team to teach school.
   c. An American anthropologist.
   d. A writer of modern novels.
   e. An American mother or father.
   f. An American grandmother or grandfather.
   g. A newly married person.
   h. A college-age student.

Compare your observation with others in class. What similarities and differences do you notice? How would you explain these similarities and differences?

6. Write a page or two in an imaginary second journal in which you comment as an observer (taking one of the roles suggested in Activity 5) of contemporary American sexual behavior of youth. What differences appear? How would you account for these differences?

6

What Influences Sexual Attitudes and Behavior?

Although sex is a biological phenomenon, inherited through the species, the attitudes and socially approved behaviors regarding sex are learned as a part of growing up in a culture, as we have seen in Chapter 5. In primitive societies this learning tends to be mainly by imitation of adults, influence of peer groups, and special rituals such as puberty rites. In more complex societies sex attitudes and moral behavior are taught by friends, family, and other social groups, and by communications media—books, newspapers, magazines, films, and pictures.

A considerable amount of discussion arises over the best ways to prepare younger generations for their sexual roles in a society. Part of the change in America referred to as a "sexual revolution" is the issue of how youth learn about sex and how they should learn. How do teen-agers acquire their sex attitudes and behaviors? This chapter offers some explanations.

1. TODAY'S CHILDREN AND SEX *

Sex education has been a subject of concern to adults for a long time. A panel of adults met to discuss the problem, and the reports of their statements are below.

---

* Reprinted by permission from *Changing Times,* the Kiplinger Magazine, June, 1966. Copyright 1966 by the Kiplinger Washington Editors, Inc., 1729 H Street, N. W., Washington, D. C. 20006.

As Old Ethics and New Freedoms Collide, What Should Grown-Ups Do?

Are you a parent? Then how do you educate your children on the subject of sex and sexual behavior? What do your children and their friends say and think among themselves?

Are you a teacher, a counselor, a social worker, a doctor, a minister? Then what are your responsibilities? Do you really understand the kids you work with?

Are you simply a concerned citizen? Then what do you make of today's young people? What will be the effect of this generation on our nation and society?

These are the problems that are under discussion in the pages that follow—a straightforward, frank clarification of a controversial and confusing subject: children and sex in today's world.

Why so much controversy and confusion? Because the older generation has been learning, to its distress, that yesterday's answers don't work any more—the younger generation is asking different questions. The younger generation has been exposed to more, knows more, is sophisticated far beyond its elders at the same age. And so the old codes have broken down, with disturbing and often ugly consequences.

This situation not only scares parents, it frequently throws many professionals for a loss, too. And that is why this discussion took place.

The Child Study Association of America—a 75-year-old nationwide voluntary agency, one of the most respected organizations in mental health education—decided to meet the problem head-on by devoting its annual conference this spring to the topic: "Sexual Behavior and Social Ethics: Their Meaning for Families Today." Translation: What should we do about children and sex? . . .

The chairman of the panel was Mildred F. Rabinow, a member of the Child Study Association staff. The panelists:

Dr. Algernon G. Black, Senior leader of the New York Society for Ethical Culture and author of *The First Book of Ethics.*

Dr. Mary S. Calderone, a physician and executive director of SEICUS, Sex Information and Education Council of the United States.

Mrs. Helen F. Southard, a psychologist and associate director of the Bureau of Research and Program Resources of the National Board, YWCA.

Dr. Saul Scheidlinger, consultant for the Community Service Society and associate clinical professor of psychology at the Albert Einstein College of Medicine.

Here is what they had to say.

Dr. Black: Every society has its moral code, and a child is brought up to believe that certain things are right or wrong. This is the accepted way to behave, this is what is expected of people. If a person violates this moral code, we consider him immoral.

But suppose he passes a judgment on the code. Suppose he says, "This is *not* moral" or "This is *not* good." He presumes to make his own value judgment. Today, we are wrestling with just such a judgment on the moral code on sex in our culture.

Many influences have broken up what formerly seemed to be a fairly set moral code. Some of them come from other countries and other cultures. But some of them come from within the cultures because the code is no longer realistic. People can no longer live by it.

With all these diverse influences, you can't just bring up people to accept a given moral code. You have to find some way of equipping them to find their *own* way. Those of us who believe in freedom must face the diversity of moral attitudes and practices—and help our children find a way of directing themselves.

I think that parents' instilling in children values by which they can make their own decisions and their own judgments as to what they will do is something that has to begin very early. It may not be a matter of talking and teaching so much as of the whole climate in the home—of respect for persons, the level and quality of relations.

In the right climate, frankness about sex and even projecting ideals of life can take place with some integrity.

Dr. Calderone: I think we need some definitions. What is sex education? I say it is an emotional and mental development continuing from the moment of birth until the end of life, through which the individual develops his sexuality as part of his total personality.

Most of sex education is negative today. Some of it is positive. Very little of it is neutral.

Next, what should be the primary goal of sex education? I think we should strive toward adults capable of using their total sexuality responsibly and creatively. The use of one's sexuality should not be limited to just one-man-one-woman relationships alone. We are relating now as sexual beings at this very instant, and have been all day.

We have not even begun to probe into the nature of sex education as a part of the whole nurturing process from birth onward. We don't even know what is "normal" sexual behavior. We only have studies, such as Kinsey's, of what people do under the influence of their culture.

If we are to change set attitudes about human sexuality, I believe that the educated middle class is the group to try to reach first. It is in this group that the phenomenon of wanting to do something to make things better, and being able to carry through on their wish, is most observable.

Dr. Scheidlinger: Yet, despite a higher delinquency rate, more drug addicts and illegitimate births, the concerns of most socially disadvantaged parents are not basically different from those of middle-class ones.

They, too, are concerned about the companions their children have, about their use of leisure time, about discipline and control and, above all, about the impact of the environment, of the public media and of street morality on sexual attitudes and behavior. The similarities in the basic concerns of all parents, regardless of cultural or economic status, by far outweigh the differences.

There is not a single social problem or distorted value in today's urban ghettos that is not present to some extent in the most advantaged neighborhoods.

Dr. Calderone: With regard to the sexual behavior of their children, I find most parents fear and are concerned about the wrong things. They don't want their daughters to get pregnant or their sons to get involved. It would be much more constructive if they directed their concern *earlier* to the chain of events that *lead* to such undesired eventualities.

It is time we began to be aware of certain factors that are important in our efforts to understand human sexual behavior today.

First, there is our tendency to equate sex with coitus. This narrow concept has succeeded in focusing our young people only on the genital and erotic aspects of sex.

Second, there is our identification of coitus as a "thing" to be exploited. In a thing-centered society, people then use sex as a thing and therefore use each other as things.

Third, there is our inability to recognize and accept the valid, and indeed the essential, sexuality of all ages from infancy on.

Fourth, there is our confusion of morality with moralisms, with these latter quite properly rejected as nonpertinent by our young people. The old moralisms are always couched in negative terms—things we should not do. But the moralities can be worded positively in terms of things we can, should want to and must do.

We do not make it clear in our schools and churches that these moralities by which human beings must live are all the same. They *have* to be the same for all relationships, whether interracial, interreligious, international or interpersonal, including sexual. That is why you can and must teach the moralities in the schools.

And fifth, there is our inability to admit to our young people that sex is a marvelous, creative, varied and colorful experience—and fun and even funny, incidentally. But this is so rare when sex is limited to the genital level—or when sex is claimed as a right before emotional maturity has earned it as a privilege.

What guidelines can parents give? At this stage in our rapidly changing society, I don't think parents are the best people to give sex—not reproductive, but sex—education to their kids. It imposes too great a burden on the parent-child relationship at a moment when it is under most stress.

I have a last suggestion: We don't give our young people the respect and attention they are entirely capable of commanding. We don't find out what they feel they need to know, who they trust to do the teaching. We have to begin the dialog and keep it open. We level with them, they level with us.

Mrs. Southard: We tend to overlook the terrific shock that it is for many parents to hear of the things that young people are saying and thinking. They tend to push it away from them. Many parents believe it is *other* people's children who are in trouble, not their own.

Many parents are concerned more about the success—and I mean success in a good sense—the ultimate happiness of their children than in the sexual difficulties that might arise along the way.

I think it is much easier for us to deal in the abstract with some of these principles than to bring them right down to reality.

Love is great when we think of love in the abstract. Love is caring. Love is family. But when it gets to the point of intimacy with 14-year-olds, then many adults run scared.

Breaking the ties of dependency is fine in the abstract. But when it comes to making a decision about having sexual relations, then has anybody talked with them about independence and what it means right down at *this* kind of breaking of parental ties?

My last point is about getting information. We have said over the years, "Learn all you can. Go out. When you are in kindergarten, go to the firehouse and ask questions. Go to the dairy. Go to all these places."

But when eighth-graders ask, "What does sexual intercourse really feel like anyhow?" some people are not prepared to answer.

I am very hopeful that those of us who believe there are strengths and learnings from our rich Judeo-Christian heritage will sift them out and be more vocal about them. I think then we will be better able to understand what sexuality is and what sex education is, and how you begin.

Dr. Black: I wonder if we could stay a little while with sex education: First, how *do* you begin this? We know that in many homes the parents are unable to deal with even the factual material of where babies come from.

The school is one place where this could begin, and part of the problem is that most schools don't do anything about it. But many of the parents would not *want* the school to do anything about it.

If you are a teacher and volunteer for it, the principal will very often say, "Well, that is up to the doctor and the nurse. Those are the people who know how to teach this." That means they want just scientific material.

I agree with Dr. Calderone that sex is not to be taken as something apart from other things. When we come to the sexual question in the ethics classes, it is part of the larger study of human relations. In those sessions there is a give and take. An atmosphere of trust, of people sharing experiences and asking questions and exchanging views, can be a very healthy atmosphere.

In every class there are children who are precocious and there are children who are maladjusted and exhibitionists. A child may ask questions in the eighth grade or seventh grade, or even earlier, which maybe one should not deal with in the group because there are children that are nowhere ready for the answers to those questions.

In the teenage years, one of the interesting discussions in sex education is, "When did you first learn about this and how did you learn about it and from whom?" One of the things that comes out is that they wish parents would begin earlier to teach them and, second, they wish that parents wouldn't be so gun-shy on questions.

But then they come to the fact that they are not sure parents should do it. They say, "Parents are overprotective. They are afraid for us. That is why we can't trust them to answer our questions as we can some other person."

Chairman Rabinow: Many of the questions we received from this audience deal with just this question. We get questions such as, "Should sex education be carried on in mixed groups?" "Is there any advantage to having separate groups?" We had several questions about what areas might be appropriate to handle in a sex education program. Why don't we begin with just a few of those.

Dr. Calderone: I have no answers because we are feeling our way, obviously. Everybody is. No teacher, no doctor, no nurse, no one person in the school should say, "These kids have got to have sex education and so I am going to do it." What a community gets in the way of sex education should be what the community wants and has been involved in preparing for. If it is what the community wants, doors are not slammed and progress will be made.

The most important thing is for the *whole* community to become involved. The whole school eventually will be involved—not only the biology and family-life teachers. The English teacher in discussing *The Scarlet Letter* will not be afraid to discuss the basic theme of the book. How was adultery looked upon at that particular epoch? How was it treated? How do we treat it today?

I think we ought to be throwing many questions to the kids. For instance, "What is marriage for?" Let them debate why marriage is still a much sought-for phenomenon in our society. "What is sex for?"

That is, besides reproduction, of course. That is a good question to throw out.

"Who makes the premarital decisions?" This is a red-hot one. It has to do with the changing relationship between men and women. The girls resent having to be the one to say no while the boys see how far they can go. The girls wonder why the boys shouldn't share in making the decision. This business of "it is the girl who can have the baby and therefore she should say no" has nothing to do with it, really.

Dr. Black: One of the interesting things to ask teenagers is, "How is sexual intercourse different from eating and drinking? Both are physical acts. But you eat and drink with anybody, you eat and drink in public. What is the difference?"

In discussing this with them, I think we must respect the sensitivities and the tenderness and the emotion as well as attempt to inform and be frank about it. I don't agree at all that it is any virtue for adults who have suddenly become emancipated to trot everything out on sensitive kids in adolescence. I think you can destroy something in them.

Dr. Scheidlinger: I think it is preposterous at this point to ask the public school system to conduct sex education because there are many teachers who, if you asked them, would say they wouldn't want to do it. I don't think any teacher should conduct sex discussions with her groups unless she wants to do it and unless she gets some help in how to do it.

I am not concerned so much about little techniques, whether one leader will be more comfortable in talking to girls alone and another with boys and girls. The question is really one of attitude. Young people today want a sense of commitment, leadership, values. The apathy that leaders so often complain about among young people is there because the leadership does not provide a commitment, a courage in terms of values.

Chairman Rabinow: I wonder if for a moment we can get back to the dilemma that occurs in families where perhaps parents would go along with many of the concepts we have talked about but are faced with the fear that they can't quite answer the questions.

One of the questions we got today was: "As a parent of a college freshman I have had a number of discussions with our daughter on sex relations and find she plans to experience sex as part of her living experience and does not think it unethical or wrong. Frankly I do not know how to cope with it."

Dr. Calderone: A lot of people have the stereotyped notion that sex education is educating about the act. That is not what I mean by sex education. I have here a letter from a very well-educated girl, a church-going girl, high in the community and her school, with lots of friends.

She says, among quite a lot of very sober and objective things, "If you have sex, you both will have a lot of fun. Sex is an active sport, more enjoyable than tennis or bowling." This is not a girl that is going to be reached by your "sensitivities" at all.

My point is that we have to start a whole lot earlier. It is too late to reach the freshman daughter because sex is a personal and private decision and, therefore, what we have to do is prepare our kids from an early age to make these personal and private decisions with all of the sensitivities that are involved. But you can't start with teenagers.

Dr. Scheidlinger: In all fairness to the mother who asked this question, I would plead that perhaps it is not too late. A single communication sometimes can carry a message of very great potential.

Suppose this mother would say, "You know, I never could have asked this question of my own mother, and you know what? It scares the dickens out of me. It scares me because I wasn't brought up at a time when one could talk freely about these things, and it scares me even more because I love you. You are my daughter, and I am afraid unless you think through some of the things you talk about, you will be hurt. So let us at least talk. I know you will make the decision because you are going off to college and nobody will be there to watch. But at least let us talk over what's involved."

Perhaps this mother will reach her daughter. I am somewhat more optimistic that it is not too late if there is a sincere dialog.

Chairman Rabinow: I think what we are saying is that perhaps we can't answer all the large questions. But we do have a responsibility to make an honest effort to answer the immediate questions that face us in our individual lives as parents and professional people.

What Do You Think?

1. How would you summarize each panelist's position on sex education?
2. Did any of the panelists state ideas with which you agree? Explain.
3. What do you think the term "sex education" should include?

2. TODAY'S CHILDREN AND SEX: WHAT READERS THINK *

A number of readers wrote to Changing Times *magazine to express their agreements or disagreements with the panel on sex education*

---

* Reprinted by permission from *Changing Times,* the Kiplinger Magazine, September, 1966. Copyright 1966 by the Kiplinger Washington Editors, Inc., 1729 H Street, N. W., Washington, D. C. 20006.

reported in the previous reading. These readers' comments appear below:

Sex education should begin early, it should begin at home, and it should be reinforced by instruction in the schools. That's the consensus of those who read "Today's Children and Sex" in the June *Changing Times* and wrote comments of their own.

But the confusion young people sense about sex today is proof aplenty that they are not getting usable guidance, either at home or at school. For that, parents accept their share of blame. Their big question is, "What do we do *now?*"

"IT'S MORE THAN SEX"

Many of the parents feel that sex is only part of the problem and that poor sex education is only a significant symptom of a general abdication of responsibility by adults.

Mrs. Richard McDowell of Boulder, Colorado, summarizes the feeling this way:

"When was the last time we had something to say to young people on codes of behavior? Clean minds? Clean bodies? When was the last time we explained to our children what is behind, and what started, and what perpetuates non-art, non-music, non-literature with its non-heroes, non-plot and non-poetry—the bankruptcy of faith from which it springs, the spiritual alienation? We're so busy talking about the new morality we've forgotten there ever was an *old* morality—that the basic moral laws in all generations through all centuries for all cultures are immutable; that civilized society is based upon certain unchanging moral laws, and that when these laws are broken or bent, the results are predictable.

"We try to pin it down—our parental dismay at what's happening to our kids—by talking about sex. It's more than sex. Sex is just the facet that worries us most. Instead of rising up in righteous indignation about any of it, we talk *to each other* about 'our children and sex' and continue to worry."

Other parents echo this call for righteous indignation. Mrs. H. W. Willingham of Paris, Tex., says: "I agree that we, the parents, must change ourselves. We must have the courage to say *no* to these children of ours, and we must start at an early age. . . . The theme of the entire discussion seemed to be that times have changed, the moral issue today is not the same as it was 20 years ago. I agree, but who changed it? Not our children, but we the adults of today, and it is up to us to call a halt to the downward trend."

The place to begin is with the very young child and in the home, according to readers. "If education in responsible thinking is to begin early, then the parents are the ones to do it," writes a Cook County, Ill., social worker, Mrs. Jerilee M. McHard. "Much is accomplished by the parents' taking the reins of educating their child in sex in the first few years. The give-and-take of early discussion strengthens the bonds of trust and respect between parent and child. If all discussion and education were left to groups and individuals outside the family, the very young child would become extremely confused, especially with regard to such abstract topics as sexual morality."

A Chicago mother, Mrs. Nicholas J. Hoeh, who began her own children's sex education when they asked their first questions, concurs and adds, "If all parents taught their children to accept sex as a part of everyday living, we would eliminate fears, shame, horror, taboo."

The idea that schools should participate in sex education raises little argument. "There is such a crying need for this material that I sometimes become impatient and perplexed at the immensity of this field," says Mrs. Dan Napuck of Neenah, Wis., "but there can be no turning back since a program *must* be instituted in our schools where we reach children from kindergarten through the twelfth grade, and where a youngster emerges as a complete human being."

Another parent, Mrs. Michael Rynas of San Francisco, calls for sex education from the first through the eighth grades, "thereby preparing a youngster to enter his teens with a well-rounded, intelligent knowledge of his sexuality, with its dual biological-emotional facets.

"It is naive and unrealistic to think that today's young adults would *not* make their own independent choice concerning sexual involvement," she says. "Wouldn't it be wiser and, indeed, beneficial to all aspects of society if they were prepared?"

But some who favor sex education in the schools wonder whether it is acceptable to other parents. "From my own experience," writes Mrs. Paul Blasi of West Concord, Mass., "I don't feel that many of the mothers would be in favor of such openness. But I do believe that the hush-hush attitudes of the past are rapidly on the wane. Even those who find such topics difficult are also finding them necessary, so it shouldn't be too long before we correct this deficiency in our children's education to the point where we can inject, and have accepted, the topic of sex in the school curriculum. Let's hope so, for the kids' sake."

There were those who spoke of the churches' share in the responsibility, too. The Rev. William E. Stirling, rector of St. Paul's Episcopal Church in Freeport, Tex., writes, "I agree wholeheartedly with the panelists. Their thoughts follow the same lines as a number of ministers have followed in this area. We have been attempting to put through a sex education course beginning with the sixth grade, following the program in the University City Public Schools, University City, Mo. I deal almost daily with unwed mothers and hasty marriages due to this lack of sex education."

BUT WHO WILL TEACH?

A Minneapolis reader raises a practical question, "Who is going to teach the teachers, and when are we going to start?"

His question is answered in part by William Bock, assistant professor of physiology and health science at Ball State University in Muncie, Ind. Dr. Bock points out that there are over 100 institutions throughout the U. S. that prepare teachers in health education. Ball State, for example, prepares teachers in health education for both elementary and secondary levels.

"It seems obvious," he says, "that the school administration should exert every effort to hire the best prepared teachers in any area, be it math, economics, or family life education. Certainly a teacher untrained and unaware of the physiological, psychological, and social implications inherent in family life education should resist such an assignment. Would you expect a history teacher to teach math? The school education health teacher is both prepared and interested in handling such an assignment."

Some health educators themselves have misgivings, however. Mrs. Rosalind Z. Goldman of West Los Angeles, a school nurse who works as a health educator, writes, "Currently I'm doing graduate work. I challenged the professor of school health education because he was pointing out the importance of health education at the *high school* level. I felt it should start at the elementary level because some of these children never get beyond the sixth grade. We have to begin where the children are—in their formative years."

Yet, despite some doubts and minor differences, the correspondents in the main agree on these essentials:

· The beginning must be made in the home, where respect for beauty, honesty, dignity, and decency, for the rights and the life and the property of others, must be taught along with the basic physiological aspects of sex.

· Parents should encourage the schools to seek out the best-trained family life educators to help bolster the training they are giving at home.

· Churches must encourage both parents and the schools to make education in sex in all its biological, psychological, and social aspects an integral part of growing into responsible adulthood.

It remained to a Wisconsin teen-ager to voice the philosophy most of the parents, teachers and clergymen seem striving to inculcate:

"When we kiss our relatives, when we shake hands, we are communicating sexually. Sex is a physical symbol of union and understanding between two people. The most sacred sex act can produce a child, an individual formed by two separate beings. Thus sex is a sacrament, an outward sign of union." She signed her letter: "An 18-year-old girl who hopes to follow her own moral code without breaking her parents'."

What Do You Think?

1. Is there a grade or age that is especially appropriate for sex education?
2. What problems in sex education have not been discussed in these two articles?
3. Do you agree with the conclusions drawn by the editors? Why or why not?
4. Will teaching children about sex largely eliminate the problems of illegitimacy and abortion? Why or why not?

3. ENLIGHTENMENT OR DEMORALIZATION? *

Must society be protected against immoral teachings? If sex attitudes and behaviors are learned from a number of sources, should there be some kind of control over material which is immoral, obscene, or pornographic? Does controlling immoral materials have any particular effect on the sexual morals of the society?

The next reading refers to the new morality in England, as shown in English literature. Is the new morality really enlightenment, or is it demoralization?

Literature and the New Morality

When I come across . . . an obvious example of the dirt-trade ["dirty" literature] masquerading as enlightened I'm inclined to be cynical about the whole of the new morality movement, with its talk about a new open communion between the sexes. Isn't it, I ask myself, significant that this compulsive preoccupation with sex has accompanied a growing crisis in the writer's situation? It's harder than ever to make a living, and the word sex sells—as we can see by looking along the shelves of any paperback shop. Hasn't the sexual revolution coincided in a significant way with various publishing crises . . . ? Hasn't the new morality been created largely by journalists who care less for principles than for keeping their own name, and their paper's name, before the public?

There are certain areas where tolerance patently does not bring the

---

* Excerpted from David Holbrook, "Enlightenment or Demoralisation?" *Twentieth Century,* Summer 1966. Reprinted by permission of the publisher. [Published in England.]

benefits claimed for it. And here, I think, we need to do some hard reconsideration, at deeper levels, of the basis of the new morality of enlightenment.

It is beginning to be obvious that one area in which mere ultra-permissiveness is not working is that of drugs. Of course it is important to ask whether authoritarian bans don't make the harmfulness of (sexy) drugs and alcohol *worse:* but it is unreal to extend this concern, to imply that it is *only* the bans or "driving underground" which cause the harm. The harm is there for all to see.

But yet there is a prevalent impulse in enlightenment to deny the evident harm. The same is happening in other spheres of concern with behaviour traditionally regarded as fraught with harm, such as sex and the depiction of sex. . . .

Such journalists . . . assume that they represent some kind of enlightened wisdom. They suggest that those who seek to restrict utterance about sex probably suffer from hidden complexes [psychological problems]. The use of the latter phrase suggests that the wisdom of these commentators is based on psychoanalytical concepts. The reference is meant to imply that because they base their "realism" on these, the writer's own attitudes must themselves be sane and complex-free. It is this kind of assumption in particular that I wish to question. I think it is a false and ignorant one. In truth, what background of study are their attitudes based on?

Perhaps I should try to make my own position as clear as I can, first. I recognize censorship as a danger, . . . but . . . I also believe that a degree of censorship is inevitable. The reason why I believe this is that I know that some human beings have an impulse to harm others, and that we all have a problem of hate. Where we all differ essentially is over the question as to whether there is hate in sex, and in the depiction of sex, and in related areas of moral enlightenment. After two years' study of psychoanalytical theory I am convinced that the prevalent attitudes of the "New Morality" are based on a disastrous failure to take into account the problem of unconscious hate.

I think the liberal mind has here become a victim of its own good-natured belief in human nature. Just as the liberal mind had the greatest difficulty in believing in the destructive evil of fascism in the thirties, it is today being misled by its innocence into accepting a process of demoralisation. This demoralisation is based not on authentic findings of psychoanalysis, or even of philosophy, but largely on the unthinking assumptions of journalistic writers. . . . What one can however suggest is that, while the ultra-permissive attitude finds easy acceptance in the press, the same press does not pay equal attention to the other less enthusiastic and more doubtful and more authentic points of view which are opposed to such writers. . . .

[There is] an attempt to persuade us that emotional realities and common values don't exist. Everywhere values are being inverted, so that serious writers can tell us that to be jealous over infidelity is uncivilized, and that we should grow out of it (Christopher Driver) or that the only criterion in sexual relationships is the hedonistic "am I happy?" (John Wilson). In reviews we are told that films and books are "enjoyably smutty" (*The Guardian*) or "brilliantly dirty" (*The Listener*): in colour supplements that "pot-and-sex" orgies are "strangely innocent" (*Weekend Telegraph*). The very valuable impulses to tolerate homosexuality and frank sexual expression are extended to false assumptions that it is wrong to regard homosexuality as deviant (Anne Douchere on *Le Batarde*) while pornography is valuable in itself (Kingsley Amis). Even to talk of curing drug addiction is impossible . . . Peter Lennon, in writing of the intellectual gangster Figon, seemed to admire the philosophical purity of his motives for murder. Wayland Young says "we must not condemn blackmail outright—it depends on who is being blackmailed." To such passes has moral relativism brought us. . . . Such moral positions are false because they deny such evidence as we have in thousands of [psychiatric] case histories that there are unconscious bases in such manifestations which mark incompletenesses of identity or splits in personality [forms of mental illness]. They also ignore the evidence that related aberrations can be at worst manifestations of the most terrible hate (as we see in the courts).

I think that today the unconscious impulses of some writers have enlisted the sincere liberal mind in promoting the creation of an ethos [1] (as over drugs and sex) in which demoralisation has reached such a pitch that a great deal of confusion, unhappiness and damage has actually been caused—as it was meant to be caused, unconsciously, by undermining the quest for identity in others, by unconscious impulses.

The prevalent impulse to bring about such a demoralisation, insofar as it is sincere, is based on a popular misunderstanding of the effect of Freudian psychoanalysis derived from his earlier theories. It is thus that the "wise are sleeping while evil is succeeding": the progressive journalistic fashion is based on phantom authorities. A suspicion of this accounts for the discomfort which many people feel about the way things are going.

As long ago as 1935 Ian D. Suttie discussed the problem of "therapeutic demoralisation" [removing restrictive attitudes to achieve better mental health]. The attitudes of the "new enlightenment" and the "new morality" are essentially based on this theoretical approach. From this point of view the therapeutic aim could be conceived in two ways: one in the postulated assurance to the patient:

---

[1] Tone, underlying spirit of a culture.

"These evil thoughts and wishes are not really bad after all. Sex is only bad for children, that is why it is hidden by adults from them. Now you are grown up and permitted to wish these things . . ."

The other is disillusion:

"Of course you are bad—if you call sex bad: we are all bad in this sense. We are merely hypocrites, and goodness is an illusion." . . .

It will be obvious to the reader that the demoralising attitudes sketched above are common bases to much in avant-garde fashionable attitudes to life and art, as expressed in the journalism of the bogus revolution, of attitudes to life to the present handful of photographers, journalists, models and fashion-peddlers who are so voluble in offering themselves as a "New British Revolution," but at a more serious level they are the implicit basis of even much that is genuine in the new morality. "We cannot really say what is right and wrong": "once we are grown up sex is only bad if we are told it is bad": "pornography only exists in 'unsophisticated' (i.e. undemoralised) minds": "morality is a mere madness of self-deceiving hypocrisy." The trouble is that in psychotherapy such mere "demoralising" does not work. If it does not work in therapeutic practice, why do we cling to it in theory and make it the basis of a "new morality"?

What Do You Think?

1. Is there a need for censorship in American society? Why? What form?
2. What is the "process of demoralization" described by the author?
3. What constitutes enlightenment in social morals?

4. IS CENSORSHIP AN ANSWER? *

Censorship of literature makes schools and libraries important areas for decisions about which written materials should be available for youth. The following article appeared as an editorial in a national journal for librarians. Does controlling "immoral materials" have any particular effect on the morals of a society?

---

* Reprinted from *School Library Journal,* April, 1966. Copyright © R. R. Bowker, 1966.

Sex Education and the Censor

When a mass-circulation magazine like *Look* devotes two features to making sex education in the schools respectable (March 8), a revolution in the teaching of sex seems clearly on its way. Add to this the emphasis on giving our teenagers more than the facts of life, apparent at recent conferences of the Child Study Association and the National Association of Independent Schools, and a new responsibility of the schools emerges —to take on what was formerly left to parents: the teaching of a personal ethic.

This imminent change in education will meet with many conservatisms —including those of school administrators, embarrassed teachers, and the not unnatural reticence of youth—who often, even when given complete freedom of reading by their parents, prefer to peruse their sex treatises under the covers with a flashlight. Whether such exploration takes place in the wake or the absence of formal teaching, an urgent concern of the librarian seems clear: to permit as wide reading as possible as the child or teenager gropes from his first curiosities to the development of individual values. This concern involves not simply books on sex and reproduction, but the encouragement of ease and self-confidence so that the child won't confront a Botticelli nude or a Michelangelo sculpture, or a descriptive or narrative passage, with nothing more than a silly leer.

The list of books prepared by the New Jersey School Library Association when it fought passage of the recent anti-smut bill (S1j, Feb. 1966, P. 54; Lj, Feb. 15, P. 1044) illuminates the range of this responsibility, as it cites the curricular areas vulnerable to extremist activity:

LITERATURE: Chaucer, *Complete Works,* any ed.; Dante, *Paradise Lost;* Tom Lea, *Hands of Cantu* (Little, Brown, 1964); John Milton, *Paradise Lost;* any ed.; *Plays of the Restoration and Eighteenth Century,* any ed.

FINE ARTS: Albert E. Elsen, *Rodin* (Museum of Modern Art; Doubleday, 1963); *Horizon Golden Book of the Renaissance* adapted for young readers by Irwin Shapiro (Golden Press, 1962); Ludwig Goldscheider, *Michelangelo* (4th ed., Phaidon, Graphic, 1962); *I, Michelangelo, Sculptor,* ed. Irving and Jean Stone (Doubleday, 1962); H. Jensen, *History of Art* (Prentice-Hall, 1962); Bernadine Kielty, *Masters of Painting* (Doubleday, 1964; o.p.).

ANTHROPOLOGY and SCIENCE: Robert J. Braidwood, *Prehistoric Men* (Chicago Natural History Museum, Oceana, 1961); Heinrich Harrer, *I Come from the Stone Age,* tr. Edward Fitzgerald (Dutton, 1965).

HISTORY and GEOGRAPHY: Erica Anderson, *World of Albert Schweitzer* (Harper, 1955); Aaron J. Erickson, ed., *The Peace Corps* (Hill and Wang, 1965); Isaac Asimov, *The Greeks: A Great Adventure* (Houghton Mifflin, 1965); Anthony Birley, *Life in Roman Britain* (Putnam, 1964); Curtis Harnack, *Persian Lambs and Persian Lions* (Holt, 1965); *Life's Picture History of Western Man* (Time, 1951, o.p.).

MYTHOLOGY: *Larousse Encyclopedia of Mythology* (Prometheus, 1959; sale by Putnam).

HEALTH and SEX EDUCATION: Karl De Schweinitz, *Growing Up* (4th ed., rev., Macmillan, 1965); Evelyn Duvall, *Why Wait Till Marriage?* (Association Press, 1965; also in approved "special Catholic edition"); Eric W. Johnson, *Love and Sex in Plain Language* (Lippincott, 1965).

PERIODICALS: *Horizon; Natural History; Unesco Courier;* and *National Geographic.*

In its accompanying statement, the NJSLA said: "There is little evidence that a free discussion of sex does any real social damage. There is overwhelming evidence that sexual ignorance brings tragic consequences to countless thousands of our young people each year. . . . [With passage of the bill] the natural curiosity of youth about the meaning and practice of sex behavior would, of necessity, be channeled to back-street information and hard-core pornography."

The hairbreadth escape of New Jersey from the anti-smut bill, just as it lay awaiting the Governor's signature, and the present efforts of New York State's schools and libraries to exempt themselves from the strictures of a similar state bill, which passed because the Intellectual Freedom Committee was sleeping, provide a cautionary tale. And the very sketchy list of books presented here should certainly disabuse any librarian of the notion that his school or children's collection would be exempt from anti-smut legislation. It is likely that the pressure for sex-education reform will increase in the coming year, as will the efforts of extremists encouraged by the recent Supreme Court decision. If this conflict is resolved in favor of the censors, which librarian will be able to call his library safe?

What Do You Think?

1. Do librarians have a responsibility in sex education?
2. Who should determine what materials are immoral or obscene or pornographic?

5. OUR UNLOVABLE SEX LAWS *

Social confusion about sexual morality is evident in the laws designed to protect the morals of citizens. This article describes the maze of laws which attempt to regulate sexual behavior and shows how the problems of sexual deviancy, pornography, contraception, and abortion are left unsolved by existing approaches.

Thanks in large part to the cheap and easy availability of contraceptive devices, to the omnipresence of the automobile (for either transportation or stationary tryst), and to more liberal community acceptance of conduct once considered beyond the pale, sexual freedom, on a private and mutually consenting level, has steadily risen throughout this century. The law, here often as archaic as it is usually impotent, has lagged farther and farther behind. One extreme example, recently in the news, involved a North Carolina statute under which a single homosexual act, even though committed in private, may be punished by imprisonment for sixty years. And this present provision is a relaxation of an older one whereby "the abominable and detestable crime against nature" might have brought a sentence of "death without the benefit of clergy."

As doctors, psychologists, sociologists, and plain observers of the sexual scene have long considered the laws against common, voluntary acts by adults more of a "crime against nature" than the acts themselves, so now the legal profession is belatedly making noises in the same direction. The U. S. Supreme Court, having finally agreed to review Connecticut's ridiculous ban on contraceptive advice (even by doctors); sales (even to married couples) and use (even by married couples), will undoubtedly declare it unconstitutional. Unconstitutional too, by several Supreme Court rulings in recent years, has been most censorship of allegedly obscene books, magazines, and motion pictures—such censorship being but an oblique legal repression of sexual expression. Most significantly, the reporters and advisors for the influential American Law Institute, in drawing up a model criminal code for the states, strongly urged, as the late Professor Fowler Harper, a pioneer in the field, recently put it, "that deviant sexual behavior between consenting adults, regardless of sex, should not constitute a criminal offense when carried on in privacy." And several states, led by Illinois, have begun to write this attitude into their laws.

Of course there are, at the other end of the scale, various forms of

* Excerpted from Fred Rodell, "Our Unlovable Sex Laws," *Trans-action,* May–June, 1968.

sex conduct that no one in his right mind would exempt from criminal penalties. Chief among these are the use of force or the threat of force to achieve sexual ends, most commonly rape, and the abuse or corruption of children by adults. Most people would also include, in this must-be-punished category, offensive sexual behavior performed in public and all forms of commercial sex or prostitution.

Yet even in the most abominated of these areas, common sense dictates a touch of caution about current laws. Thus, both rape and the abuse of minors are combined in the concept of statutory rape—or intercourse, however unforced or even invited, with a girl younger than the "age of consent." But the age of consent, varying in different states from as low as 14 to as high as 21, usually hovers around 16 or 18. This means that for almost every pregnant high-school girl (and their increasing numbers have been called a national scandal)—as well as for almost every unvirginal but more careful high-school girl—there is, technically, a rapist presumably at large. . . .

Similarly, some of our laws making crimes of comparatively minor sex acts or gestures—because committed in public—may be too extreme and may also be discriminatory. Such laws directed against exhibitionists, voyeurs (or peeping Toms), and frotteurs (who rub against strangers in subways or other crowded places) are rarely applied to women, who may be just as guilty as men. As one lady lawyer, Harriet Pilpel, has gallantly pointed out, a man caught watching through a window while a woman undresses may be arrested as a voyeur, whereas if the sexes are reversed it is the undressing man who may be held as an exhibitionist. Likewise, laws against blatant public displays of homosexuality are almost always enforced only against men.

But where homosexuals ply their partner-seeking overtly in public, the offensiveness may be no less than that of street-walkers, even though money may not be its aim. As for prostitution itself (along with its manservant, so to speak, procuring) not without reason is it known as the oldest profession. In no place and at no time in history have laws prohibiting it proved effective, although regulation and licensing have sometimes served to control it and so diminish its more dangerous consequences, such as disease and corruption of police.

A LEGISLATIVE JUNGLE

It would be impossible, in a short space, to list all [the] in-between sex laws which, in our current culture, may be deemed dubious, unnecessary, or silly. They range from a North Carolina statute prohibiting any "act of lewdness" with a student "within three miles of a school or college" (but, by negative implication, not if four miles away) to a Vermont law that forbids the advertising of any drug as a cure for venereal disease (which apparently lumps together effective drugs and quack concoctions). Yet a few of these laws deserve a word—because they are venerable, well-nigh universal, and, as our sex habits and attitudes relax, increasingly controversial.

Although only two states completely outlaw birth-control by mechanical means (other states regulate advertising and place of sale of contraceptives), abortion—contraception's dangerous handmaiden and one of the nation's major sociomedical problems—is everywhere a crime which may be punished by as many as fifteen years in prison or, if the mother dies, even as murder. Most states make an exception if abortion is needed to save the mother's life, but not merely to save her physical or mental health. Indeed, no state even legalizes an abortion because pregnancy was caused by rape. And the restrictions on legal abortions performed in hospitals by qualified doctors—usually disguised under a less ugly name as "d and c" (dilation and curettage)—are stringent.

The well-known result of these rigid laws is the wide prevalence of illegal abortions performed in unsanitary surroundings by incompetent members of "abortion mills" for exorbitant fees—as well as the shockingly high proportion of deaths. Estimates of the number of illegal abortions performed in the U. S. run as high as a million a year, with not one in a thousand ever prosecuted. It is because of this almost total breakdown in the effective enforcement of abortion laws—as well as for humanitarian reasons—that one of the proposals of the American Law Institute's model code would drastically relax present bans against legal abortions. And for those moralists who may fear that such relaxation would further encourage pre-marital or extra-marital sex, be aware that one expert has estimated that 90 per cent of U. S. illegal abortions are performed on married women with three or more children, which would put the number of unwed near-mothers seeking illegal relief from pregnancy well below 10 per cent of the total. . . .

A final quartet of sex crimes, all of them centered around marriage, are bigamy, incest, seduction, and miscegenation. Bigamy must of course be forbidden in a monogamous nation. Yet the present tangle of conflicting divorce laws and requirements—coupled with the ease and popularity of peripatetic divorce—may make many a man an unwitting bigamist. Further, innocent divorce-based bigamy is almost never prosecuted except at the insistence of a supposed exwife out for money (to buy her off) or revenge. What is needed here is not a change in the bigamy laws but a reform of the confusion of divorce laws.

Despite the fact that Cleopatra married two of her brothers (no bigamist, she married them consecutively), incest has been taboo in most societies down through the ages and is so in the U. S. today, although different states define the crime slightly differently; first cousins living in Iowa would have to move across the state line to Minnesota to be married. Not only marriage but extramarital intercourse by close relatives is heavily punished in many states. Where the banning of such unions is based on blood relationship, laws against incest make genetic sense (although inbreeding of animals is often favored); but where, as in several states, incest is stretched to cover in-laws and stepchildren, it betrays a religious root which is largely outdated today.

Largely outdated too in the light of current sex mores, but still on most statute books is the old crime of seduction—or persuading a girl or woman to have intercourse by a promise of marriage. Suffice it to note here that the lady must be virgin at the time of seduction, that it must be the promise, nothing else, that leads her to comply, and that the man must make the promise with deliberate intent to deceive—all rather difficult points to prove when the villain later backs away from the altar.

As for miscegenation, prohibited in very few places outside the U. S. and by barely over half of our states, the laws making it criminal are likely on their way out, courtesy of the judiciary. The California Supreme Court has declared unconstitutional that state's legal bar on interracial marriage. And only this winter, the U. S. Supreme Court vetoed a Florida ban on interracial extra-marital intercourse, while at least hinting that, when a proper case came before it, it might throw out a typical anti-miscegenation-in-marriage statute (and thus, by inference, all such statutes) as well.

Yet the task of bringing most of our sex laws up to date with our liberalized sex beliefs and sex behavior—of narrowing if not closing the hypocritical chasm between what we purport to forbid and what we do—is primarily and properly the job of the legislators, not judges. This is what the American Law Institute's model code recognizes—and urges on the states. Not that these lawyers, backed by psychiatrists and other professional groups, are advocating an officially authorized loosening of sexual morals; they would simply have our outmoded sex-crime laws reformed—or in some instances, repealed—instead of regularly broken and ignored. And where legitimate private, as opposed to public, interests are still at stake, the law would still protect them, thus, adultery would remain a ground for divorce but not a crime.

It is a cliché that we cannot legislate morality. Even less can we legislate effectively against conduct which a large part of the community has come to accept as not immoral.

What Do You Think?

1. What laws are needed for sexual behaviors?
2. How can appropriate laws be enforced?
3. Can morality be legislated?

4. Is it possible to define deviancy and pornography in clear, legal terms that are reasonable and modern?

ACTIVITIES FOR INVOLVEMENT

1. Make a list of all sources of sex information available to teen-agers. Place each source in order from the most helpful to the least helpful. Compare your list with others in the class. What criteria were used in judging helpfulness?

2. Using the total class list of sources of sex information, rate each source according to its potential for improving the sexual attitudes and behaviors of teen-agers. Place the source which you think has the highest potential for improving teen-agers at the top, the lowest potential at the bottom. Compare this list with the one from item 1 on helpfulness. Are they different? If so, how would you account for this?

3. Read the following summaries of newspaper articles:

a. A jury in London found the novel "Last Exit to Brooklyn," by Hubert Selby Jr., obscene. This novel has not met "noticeable opposition from the waning forces of censorship in the United States, where it has sold freely." Frank Kermode, previously a co-editor of *Encounter* magazine, said that the book was "very much in the tradition of Dickens, who spoke of shame, misery, and degradation of a great capital." Sir Basil Blackwell, owner of Blackwell's book shop, said the book was "all one thing—abominable thoughts, abominable words, and abominable conduct." He added that it "depraved" him and "defiled his mind." (Reported in *The New York Times,* Nov. 24, 1967.)

b. Anson Mount, public affairs manager of Playboy Enterprises, stated that sex "is immoral only when it interferes with human welfare and happiness." He further maintained that the moralists of today's world have a "demonic view of sexuality," adding that "Human sexuality to these people is a beast that must be closely policed." (Reported in *Buffalo Evening News,* March 21, 1968.)

c. The Citizens for Decent Literature, a group dedicated to "wholesome" literature, indicated to the Supreme Court that the Court's recent obscenity decisions had "opened the flood gates on a deluge of new pornography." They noted increases in juvenile delinquency and illegitimate births and requested the Justices to return to the rationale used in upholding the conviction of Ralph Ginzburg, publisher of a magazine. The friend-of-the-court brief in which this position was expressed referred to 22 obscenity convictions from lower courts which had been reversed by the Supreme Court. (Reported in *The New York Times,* Nov. 23, 1967.)

Write a brief paper in which you attempt to explain any one of the views presented. Support your explanation with additional evidence from books, magazines, papers, friends, parents, or other sources.

4. Conduct a mock trial of a classmate accused of corrupting the morals of youth by selling modern novels. Appoint one student as prosecutor, one as defense attorney, and some students as witnesses. The teacher will

act as judge, and the class will act as jury. Outline the charges specifically, call "expert" witnesses to testify on the present state of morality in society, the book(s) in question, and aspects of censorship.

5. Hold a class discussion on the subject:
Some censorship is necessary in any civilized society.

BIBLIOGRAPHY
For Further Study

Books

CALHOUN, ARTHUR W. · *A Social History of the American Family* · New York, N. Y.: Barnes and Noble, Inc., 1917, 1945.

CALVERTON, W. F., and SCHMALHAUSEN, S. D. (eds.) · *Sex in Civilization* · Garden City, N. Y.: Garden City Publishers, 1929.

COLE, WILLIAM G. · *Sex and Love in the Bible* · New York, N. Y.: Association Press, 1959.

COMFORT, ALEX · *Sexual Behavior in Society* · New York, N. Y.: Viking Press, 1950.

DAVIS, MAXINE · *Sex and the Adolescent* · New York, N. Y.: Dial Press, 1958.

DUVALL, EVELYN and SYLVANUS (eds.) · *Sex Ways—In Fact and Faith* · New York, N. Y.: Association Press, 1961.

DUVALL, EVELYN · *Why Wait Till Marriage?* · New York, N. Y.: Association Press, 1965.

DUVALL, EVELYN and JOHNSON, JOY · *The Art of Dating* · New York, N. Y.: Association Press, 1967.

DONIGER, SIMON (ed.) · *Sex and Religion Today* · New York, N. Y.: Association Press, 1953.

ELLIS, A. · *The Folklore of Sex* · New York, N. Y.: Chas. Bondi, 1951.

FITCH, ROBERT E. · *The Decline and Fall of Sex* · New York, N. Y.: Harcourt, Brace & World, 1951, 1956, 1957.

FROMM, ERICH · *The Art of Loving* · New York, N. Y.: Harper & Row, 1956.

GRIMM, ROBERT · *Love and Sexuality* · New York, N. Y.: Association Press, 1964.

HULME, WILLIAM · *God, Sex and Youth* · Englewood Cliffs, N. J.: Prentice-Hall, Inc., 1959.

JOHNSON, ERIC W. · *Love and Sex in Plain Language* · Phila., Pa.: J. B. Lippincott Co., 1965, 1967.

LEUBA, CLARENCE · *The Ethics of Sex Conduct* · New York, N.Y.: Association Press, 1948.

LINDSAY, BENJAMIN and EVANS, WAINWRIGHT · *The Revolt of Modern Youth* · New York, N. Y.: Boni and Liveright, 1925.

LORAND, RHODA L. · *Love, Sex and the Teen Ager* · New York, N. Y.: The Macmillan Co., 1965.

PIKE, JAMES A. · *Teen-Agers and Sex: A Guide for Parents* · Englewood Cliffs, N. J.: Prentice-Hall, Inc., 1965.

REICH, WILHEIM · *The Sexual Revolution* · Tr. by Theo. Wolfe · New York, N. Y.: Orgone Institute Press, 1945.

REISS, IRA L · *Premarital Sex Standards in America* · New York, N. Y.: Free Press of Glencoe, 1960.

RUSSELL, BERTRAND · *Marriage and Morals* · New York, N. Y.: Liveright, 1929.

TRIMBOS, C. J. · *Healthy Attitude Towards Love and Sex* · Tr. by Geofrey Chapman · New York, N. Y.: P. J. Kenedy & Sons, 1962, 1964.

WESTERMARCK, EDWARD · *A Short History of Marriage* · London, Eng.: The Macmillan Co., 1926.

Pamphlets

American Medical Association (Sex Education Series), Chicago, Ill.

LERRIGO and SOUTHARD · *Facts Aren't Enough; Finding Yourself; Approaching Adulthood.*

American Social Health Association, New York, N. Y.

CORNER · *Attaining Manhood; Attaining Womanhood.*
ENGLISH and FINCH · *Emotional Problems of Growing Up.*
DUVALL · *Facts of Life and Love for Teen-Agers; Know Your Daughter and Know Your Son.*
STRAIN · *New Patterns in Sex Teaching.*
BARUCH · *New Ways in Sex Education.*
KIRKENDALL · *Understanding Sex.*

E. C. Brown Trust, Portland, Ore.

DUBBE · *What Do Your Adolescents Tell You?*
KIRKENDALL · *Sex Concerns of Adolescent Boys.*

Child Study Association of America, *When Children Ask About Sex.* New York, N. Y.

Family Life Publications, Durham, N. C.

BECK · *Human Growth.*
RICHARDSON · *For Teen-Agers Only.*
PEMBERTON · *The Stork Didn't Bring You.*

Public Affairs Committee, New York, N. Y.
KIRKENDALL and OGG · *Sex and Our Society.*

Paperback Books

DUVALL, EVELYN M. · *Facts of Life and Love for Teen-Agers* · New York, N. Y.: Popular Library, 1957.

HYLME, WILLIAM · *Youth Considers Sex* · Youth Forum Series, Camden, N. J.: Thomas Nelson & Sons, 1966.

JAFFÉ, GABRIEL · *Promiscuity* · New York, N. Y.: Dell, 1966.

MACE, DAVID R. · *Youth Considers Marriage* · Youth Forum Series, Camden, N. J.: Thomas Nelson & Sons, 1966.

POPENOE, PAUL · *Sex, Love and Marriage* · New York, N. Y.: Belmont Books, 1963.

WHITE, PATRICIA and CHRISTINE · *To Love Is to Grow* · New York, N. Y.: Abingdon Press, 1962.

WEATHERHEAD, LESLIE D. · *The Mastery of Sex* · New York, N. Y.: Abingdon Press, 1959.

WILSON, JOHN · *Logic and Sexual Morality* · Baltimore, Md.: Penguin Books, 1965.

Articles

BELL, ROBERT and BLUMBERG, LEON · "Courtship and Intimacy Attitudes," *The Family Life Coordinator,* March 1960.

BUERKLE, JACK · "Mother and Daughter Attitudes Toward Premarital Sexual Behavior," *Marriage and Family Living,* November 1961.

BERNARD, JESSIE · "The Fourth Revolution," *Journal of Social Issues,* April 1966.

BLOOD, ROBERT · "Romance and Premarital Intercourse—Incompatibles?", *Marriage and Family Living,* May 1952.

BRODERICK, CARLFRED and FOWLER, STANLEY · "New Patterns of Relationship Between the Sexes Among Preadolescents," *Marriage and Family Living,* February 1961.

CAREY, REV. JAMES A. · "What Happened When My School Banned Going Steady," *McCall's Magazine,* June 1963.

CHRISTENSEN, HAROLD T. · "Dating Behavior As Evaluated by High School Students," *The American Journal of Sociology,* May 1952. "Cultural Relativism and Premarital Sex Norms," *American Sociological Review,* February 1960. "Scandinavian and American Sex Norms: Comparisons With Sociological Implications," *Journal of Social Issues,* April 1966.

DUNN, MARIE · "Marriage Role Expectations of Adolescents," *Marriage and Family Living,* May 1960.

DUVALL, EVELYN · "Adolescent Love as a Reflection of Teen-Agers Search for

Identity," *Journal of Marriage and the Family,* May 1964. "Exploring Student Attitudes About Dating," *Journal of Home Economics,* February 1964.

EHRMANN, WINSTON · "Changing Sex Mores," in *Reference Papers on Children and Youth,* Golden Anniversary White House Conference on Children and Youth, 1960.

FISCHER, JOHN · "The Harm Good People Do," *Harper's Magazine,* October 1956.

GLASSBERG, BERT · "Sexual Behavior Patterns in Contemporary Youth Culture —Implications for Later Marriage," *Journal of Marriage and the Family,* May 1965

GOODMAN, WALTER · "The New Sex Education," *Redbook Magazine,* September 1967.

JAMESON, STORM · "Love's Labors Exposed," *Atlas Magazine,* July 1966.

KNUDSEN, DEAN, POPE, HALLOWELL, and IRISH, DONALD · "Response Differences to Questions on Sexual Standards: An Interview—Questionnaire Comparison," *Public Opinion Quarterly,* Summer 1967.

MILAS, SUZANNE · "Why I Believe in Sex Before Marriage," *Redbook Magazine,* November 1967.

MURRAY, JOHN C. · "The Bad Arguments Intelligent People Make," *America,* November 3, 1956.

SILBERMAN, ARLENE · "The Pregnant Bride," *Redbook Magazine,* November 1966.

"Sweden's Sexocracy," *Atlas Magazine,* December 1966.

VINCENT, CLARK · "Teen-age Unwed Mothers in American Society," *Journal of Social Issues,* April 1966.

WASSMER, THOMAS · "The New Morality: Some Questions," *America,* August 5, 1967.

WELLS, H. G. · "Mankind in the Making: Love and the Cultivation of the Imagination," *Cosmopolitan,* June 1903.

Films and Tapes

Boy to Man (16 min; color; Churchill Films, 1961) · Diagrams show physical changes in adolescent boys and differences in growth patterns. Venice Film Festival Award Winner.

From Generation to Generation (30 min; color; McGraw-Hill, 1959) · A Columbus Film Festival Award Winner showing childbirth as an emotional and spiritual experience in addition to its acceptance as a part of the natural order.

Going Steady? (41 fr; McGraw-Hill) · Presents problems in steady dating for adolescents.

Going Steady (Tape; 15 min; Purdue Univ.) · Partly dramatized radio show. Presents concepts of going steady in terms of school and friends.

How Free Are You? (75 fr; sound coordinated on record; color; Methodist Church, Wash. D. C.) • Designed as discussion aid on topics of gambling, narcotics, alcohol, and pornography. Poses questions of morality.

How Much Affection (20 min; B/W; McGraw-Hill) • Story of a young couple going steady. Develops problems of petting, affection, level of involvement.

How to Act on a Date (44 fr; with sound recording; Family Films, 1958) • Shows the teen-ager how to prepare for a date, maintaining standards of conduct. Discussion topics at end of record.

Human Beginnings (22 min; color; Associated Films) • A sex education film for very young (first grade) children.

Human Reproduction (23 min; B/W; McGraw-Hill, 1948) • An old, but complete film originally designed for college courses on the topic of reproduction. Well-done treatment of male and female development. A filmstrip is also available.

Human Relations (29 min; B/W; Carousel Films) • Problems of dating, going steady, parents, premarital sex. Presents view that sex is part of societal life.

Human Growth (20 min; color, Health Education Service, 1948) • Deals with reproduction and puberty changes using 7th grade classroom as location. Menstruation, body changes, secondary sex characteristics and sex organ development are clearly explained. A filmstrip and text are also available.

Is Sex Education a Function of the Schools? (Tape; 30 min; Univ. of Colorado, National Tape Repository) • A discussion tape on the public school position on sex education.

Meaning of Adolescence (16 min; color; McGraw-Hill) • Deals with parents and teen-agers in adjustment to adult life. Treats topics of physical change, getting along with the opposite sex, and making moral decisions.

Name Unknown (10 min; color; Sid Davis Productions, Hollywood) • Shows sex criminal and how he works on a teen-ager in a series of episodes including lovers lane, baby sitting, and pick up.

Sex Education: About Play and Masturbation (Tape; 9 min; Univ. of Colorado, National Tape Repository) • Dr. Helen Bull presents a discussion on early childhoood and the value of sex education.

Sex Education: Preparation for Adolescence (Tape; 10 min; Univ. of Colorado, National Tape Repository) • Dr. Helen Bull suggests ways parents can assist children to understand the physical changes of adolescence.

Social-Sex Attitudes in Adolescence, (22 min; B/W; McGraw-Hill) • Shows life stories of young marrieds. Compares sex education, adjustment in adolescence, influences.

The Playboy and the Christian (2 Kinescopes, 27 min ea; Carousel Films) • These films are from the CBS Television show, "Look Up and Live." They feature Harvey Cox and use religious positions in dealing with morality.

When Are We Ready for Marriage? (37 fr; color; Script and Guide, Popular Science Publishing Co., N. Y.) · Encourages thought before marriage for young people. Attention called to practical considerations, but spiritual motif is underlying.

Who Should Decide? (11 min; color; Coronet Films, 1958) · Presents typical problem areas between parents and teen-agers. Raises questions of extent of parental control.